D1139189

this is
GLUTEN-FREE

this is GLUTEN-FREE

Delicious gluten-free recipes to bake it better

VICTORIA HALL

Photography by Adrian Lawrence

RYLAND PETERS & SMALL
LONDON • NEW YORK

Senior designer Sonya Nathoo
Commissioning editor Stephanie Milner
Head of Production Patricia Harrington
Art director Leslie Harrington
Editorial director Julia Charles
Publisher Cindy Richards

Food stylists Victoria Hall and Jack Sargeson
Prop stylists Jennifer Kay and Luis Peral
Indexer Vanessa Bird

First published in 2017 by
Ryland Peters & Small
20–21 Jockey's Fields, London WC1R 4BW
and
341 E 116th St, New York NY 10029

www.rylandpeters.com

10 9 8 7 6 5 4 3 2 1

Text copyright © Victoria Hall 2017

Design and photographs copyright ©
Ryland Peters & Small 2017

ISBN: 978-1-84975-811-6

Printed in China

A CIP record for this book is available from the British
Library.

US Library of Congress Cataloging-in-Publication Data
has been applied for.

Disclaimer:
The views expressed in this book are those of the
author but they are general views only and readers are
urged to consult a relevant and qualified specialist or
physician for individual advice before beginning any
dietary regimen. Ryland Peters & Small hereby exclude
all liability to the extent permitted by law for any errors
or omissions in this book and for any loss, damage or
expense (whether direct or indirect) suffered by a third
party relying on any information contained in this book.
You should always consult your physician before
changing your dietary regimen.

Notes:

• Successful gluten-free baking requires accuracy
in measuring ingredients. Some ingredients used
within the recipes in this book are accurate to the
nearest gram, millilitre and quarter-ounce. You should
invest in good-quality digital scales for weighing
ingredients and for best results.

• Both British (Metric) and American (Imperial plus
US cups) measurements are included in these recipes
for convenience; however it is important to work with
one set of measurements and not alternate between
the two within a recipe.

• All spoon measurements are level unless otherwise
specified.

• All eggs are large (UK) or extra-large (US), unless
specified as large, in which case US extra-large should
be used. Uncooked or partially cooked eggs should not
be served to the very old, frail, young children,
pregnant women or those with compromised immune
systems.

• Ovens should be preheated to the specified
temperatures. We recommend using an oven
thermometer. If using a fan-assisted oven, adjust
temperatures according to the manufacturer's
instructions.

• When a recipe calls for the grated zest of citrus fruit,
buy unwaxed fruit and wash well before using. If you
can only find treated fruit, scrub well in warm soapy
water before using.

• When a recipe calls for baking powder, bicarbonate
of/baking soda and other such standard baking
ingredients, check that they have been manufactured
in a gluten-free environment.

• There are certain healthy risk associated with
whipped cream so always practice food safety by using
fresh cream before it's expiry date and covering and
storing prepared cakes and desserts in the fridge until
ready to serve.

• To sterilize preserving jars, wash them in hot,
soapy water and rinse in boiling water. Preheat the
oven to 160°C (325°F) Gas 3. Dry the jars well with a
clean kitchen cloth, then put into the oven, on a baking
sheet for 10 minutes. Remove and allow to cool before
filling. Alternatively, if you have a dishwasher, empty it
completely and then run the jars through on the highest
heat setting. Remove just before filling. Sterilize the
lids for 5 minutes, by boiling or according to the
manufacturer's instructions. Jars should be filled and
sealed while they are still hot.

Contents

Introduction 6

Basic Ingredients 8

Equipment and Storage 13

Basic Techniques 14

Basic Pastry 16

Fillings and Sauces 18

Small Bakes and Cupcakes 20

Larger Cakes 58

Perfect Pastry 80

Delicious Desserts 108

Savoury Bakes 140

Suppliers and Resources 156

Index 158

Acknowledgments 160

introduction

I'm sure I can't remember the first time I baked a cake. I, like most, have vivid recollections of baking with my Mum and sisters on rainy afternoons and I can recall some spectacular birthday cakes from my childhood, but I didn't grow up harbouring ambitions to become a baker. Baking was, honestly, a very occasional activity.

Discovering that I could no longer eat gluten during my first year of university changed all that. Suddenly, I couldn't just shop and eat with abandon and instead found myself spending hours in the supermarket deciphering ingredients labels, only to be disappointed at just how many things I could no longer enjoy. It was 2005 and the 'free-from' offerings were scarce. Surrounded by friends in student digs tucking into shop-bought sweet treats, I realised that if I too wanted to indulge, I was going to have to do something about it myself.

With a forgiving lecture schedule, and plenty of willing guinea-pigs, my student kitchen quickly became a testing ground for cakes, cookies, muffins, brownies and traybakes. Friends knew that whatever the day, there'd be something either just about to go into, or just about to come out of the oven. At one stage, I covered an entire wall of our kitchen with recipes torn from cookery magazines that I wanted to adapt over the coming semesters. For a decade, baking was an almost daily pasttime. I didn't need a reason, I just loved the challenge of mastering a recipe and making it gluten-free. I had developed something of an obsession.

Despite completing my training as a speech and language therapist and taking a role in London, it was becoming obvious that my passion lay elsewhere. After a particularly industrious Saturday in the kitchen, resulting in three types of cupcakes, baked for no real reason at all, a quiet suggestion; 'Why don't you try to sell these cakes?' was enough to spark an ambitious plan. I looked into how and where I could sell my cakes and subsequently set up an online cupcake business, which swiftly took off and soon, I was delivering gluten-free cupcakes to Whole Foods Market three times a week and running stalls at pop-up food markets.

Working full-time, baking almost every night and delivering most mornings, it didn't take long for me to realize I needed to seriously focus on one or the other. Baking won, hands down, and I set up a fully fledged 100% gluten-free restaurant. The risk of cross-contamination when eating out was too serious an issue to ignore, there was a clear gap in the market and one can't live on cake alone. After finding a beautiful Victorian townhouse in the centre of Leeds, back in my home county of Yorkshire, and instantly falling in love with it, I handed in my notice, dedicated over a year to perfecting my baking, and enrolled in a cookery course at Leith's. My parents were unbelievably supportive and it's thanks to them that we opened 2 Oxford Place.

And oh, what a shock it was! Transitioning to baking full-time to run the restaurant meant budgets that forced me to develop recipes as efficient as they were tasty. And that worked. Every time. Very much in at the deep end and learning on the job, I was speaking every day to people with varied dietary requirements and hearing so often that their kitchens had become a battleground. Once easily navigated and commanded, they were now an environment full of hidden, hostile ingredients and a scene for unpredictable and often inedible results. Customers would ask daily for one recipe or another.

After about a year of running the restaurant, and with some critical acclaim under our belts, I got to thinking, wasn't it about time to put pen to paper and finally respond properly to the customer demand for recipes? So here were are. I'm delighted to showcase a collection of my gluten-free baking recipes and I really hope that this book will prove a useful resource for anyone looking to bake without gluten. With a bit of practice, everything can be adapted, without compromise on taste or texture, I promise. But don't just take my word for it – the proof is, as they say, in the pudding. Happy baking!

basic ingredients

It is the constant refrain of cookery shows and writers; the end result is only as good as the ingredients you put in. It's true, but for baking this really doesn't mean spending a fortune. In fact, as long as you use the right ingredients, you can buy budget and still produce amazing bakes. Not only this, but take care to use them properly. Fridge-cold butter just isn't going to work in your cake, whether it is value range or handmade in the Alpine foothills. For baking without gluten there are a couple of specialist ingredients that need to become your store-cupboard staples. They are easy to find and used in small quantities; embrace them and you will see your treats transformed.

Baking powder

Essentially a mixture of sodium bicarbonate and cream of tartar, baking powder is used to aerate a mixture when heated. It is responsible for the rise in your cakes when they go into the oven. It is important to ensure that the baking powder you buy is gluten-free as they can be bulked with wheat starch. Any baking powders marked as 'gluten-free' or with only cornstarch/cornflour or rice flour listed as additions in the ingredients are absolutely fine.

I like to use Doves Farm baking powder, and the measurements in this book refer to this particular brand. Despite only being used in small amounts, different brands can produce different results, so if your bakes rise too much or too little, simply up or lower the amount used by a gram or two.

Alternatively, you can blend your own baking powder by mixing 4 teaspoons of cream of tartar with 2 teaspoons of bicarbonate of soda/baking soda. Combine thoroughly and use the quantity as directed in the recipe.

Bicarbonate of soda/Baking soda

This is a component of baking powder. It serves the same purpose of leavening bakes. The key difference between the two is that baking powder already has an acidic element added into it, meaning all it needs to work is moisture and heat.

When using bicarbonate of soda/baking soda, it is necessary to introduce that acidic element into the recipe onself. A great example of this is the addition of buttermilk to red velvet cupcakes.

Bicarbonate of soda/baking soda does have a 'tangy' taste that you won't find with baking powder. Be careful not to use too much, or you can overpower the flavour of the bake.

Because bicarbonate of soda/baking soda will begin to react as soon as it meets its acidic helper, it's important to work quickly with these batters, and get them into the oven as soon as possible.

Butter

Churned from milk or cream, butter is the mainstay of a great many baking recipes. The recipes in this book call for unsalted butter – be sure not to buy salted or slightly salted as this will affect the taste of your bakes. Also remember that the butter you are going to want to use to bake with will be different from the butter you are using for spreading on your toast in the morning. Bear in mind that butters all have unique flavours which will impart themselves in your finished bake.

Find a butter that is neutral in flavour – this is likely to be one of the cheaper options. Particularly when making frostings, an expensive butter with a very pronounced 'buttery' taste will be detectable, which is not the desired outcome. If you are buying butter for serving alongside your bakes, such as with scones, of course pick whichever has the flavour which appeals to you most.

It's really important for most bakes that butter is at room temperature, in order that it can be incorporated with the other ingredients correctly. Take the butter out of the fridge at least a couple of hours before using it, or the night before, to allow it to come up to temperature and soften slightly. If you have forgotten to do so, cut the amount required from the chilled block and microwave on half power for 10–20 seconds to soften it up.

Buttermilk

This is a low fat milk product. Although now commercially produced, traditionally it was the liquid leftover when cream was churned into butter.

As it is slightly acidic, it is used in conjunction with a raising agent to produce air and create lift in a bake.

If you can't find any buttermilk in your local store or you have run out, you can make your own with a bit of elbow grease. Take a carton of double/heavy cream and a larger empty plastic milk carton. Pour the cream into the milk carton and shake vigorously until the cream separates into butter and buttermilk. Keep shaking until you have a solid block of butter in the carton and then pour out the buttermilk for use in your recipe.

Chocolate

The most common chocolate used in baking is dark/bittersweet, as the flavour marries well with the sweet ingredients it is being used alongside. It also melts more easily, being less prone to burning, because of the lower sugar content. Be sure to buy dark/bittersweet chocolate with at least 50% cocoa solids, but don't choose chocolate with a cocoa solid percentage higher than 70%. Buy good-quality chocolate wherever possible, and avoid chocolate labelled as 'cooking' or 'coating' as these will have added oils which may affect the taste and texture of your bake.

When adding chocolate chips to recipes, you can either buy ready chipped dark/bittersweet, milk/semi-sweet or white chocolate, and in contrast, these may be labelled 'for cooking', which is fine. As the chips are not being mixed with the other ingredients, but rather standing alone within a scone, cake or cookie, they won't affect the overall texture of the bake. If you prefer, you can chop a bar of chocolate into chunks instead.

Cocoa

Cocoa powder is used to add chocolate flavour to bakes, without the need for melted chocolate, or to enhance flavour alongside it. Cocoa powder is very different to hot chocolate powder which contains sugar and sometimes milk powder, so look for 100% cocoa. For US bakers, if the recipe is mostly leavened by bicarbonate of soda/baking soda, reach for Dutch-processed cocoa; if it uses baking soda, go for natural cocoa powder.

Colours

Adding food colourings is sometimes required (see Red Velvet Cake, page 63) and sometimes an optional, fun extra. I recommend using gel food colourings as they are concentrated and so impart a vibrant hue without needing to use too much, which could affect the taste or texture of your baking. They also retain their colour during baking, whereas some liquid colours can fade when heated. It is important to check that the colours and any other edible decorations that you buy are gluten-free – colours typically are, but quite often sprinkles are not.

Cream, double/heavy

This is a thick cream with a high fat content that can be whipped until stiff. If you are unable to find double/heavy cream for filling a cake or roulade, you can substitute whipping cream, but do not make substitutions if the cream is to be baked into a recipe.

Cream, single/light

This is a lower fat and much thinner type of cream and cannot be substituted for double/heavy cream in recipes. It is good for pouring over bakes.

Dairy-free spreads

Dairy-free butter alternatives are most commonly made from sunflower oil, olive oil or soya and are readily available in the supermarket. As when baking with butter, find a neutral-flavoured spread as you don't want the taste to be too pronounced in the final bake. Keep your dairy-free spreads in the fridge, and as they are much softer than butter there is no need to bring them up to room temperature before using.

Dried and candied fruits

Dried fruits such as sultanas/golden raisins, dates, dark raisins and candied fruits like mixed peel and glacé cherries are all commonplace in traditional bakes. For fruit cakes and Christmas puddings, the fruits will benefit from overnight soaking before using – either in alcohol or fruit juice – to ensure that they are plump and moist in the bake. There is no need to soak the fruits before adding to quick bakes such as scones.

Be careful to check your dried fruits are gluten-free. Sultanas/golden raisins, dark raisins, currants and cranberries usually are. Dates and dried apricots may be tossed in a starch containing gluten to preserve them, but you can easily find ones that have not been. Mixed peel and glacé cherries, and other fruits that have been candied may have wheat starch in the syrup, which is not gluten-free, search out brands without this additive.

Eggs

Use UK large/US extra-large eggs for all of the recipes in this book. Keep them outside of the fridge at room temperature wherever possible. If a recipe calls for egg yolks only – use the whites to make meringue as this will keep for far longer than the egg whites themselves. If a recipe calls for egg whites only, the yolks can be made into custard.

Flour, corn/cornstarch

Cornflour/cornstarch is a very fine white flour that is naturally gluten-free. Be sure to use cornflour/cornstarch that fits this description rather than coarse cornmeal. You will likely find cornflour/cornstarch among the regular flours or near to the powdered gravy and spices as it is commonly used for thickening sauces in savoury cooking. I like to add a little to whipped cream to stabilize it and prevent the moisture leaching into a bake.

Flour, plain/all-purpose

Gluten-free plain/all-purpose flour is a blend of naturally gluten-free flours and starches, typically tapioca, potato, corn and rice, and possible buckwheat or sorghum. The recipes in this book all call for plain/all-purpose gluten-free flour rather than self-raising/rising as this allows you to add the correct amount of leavening agent and xanthan gum yourself, according to each individual bake. I use Doves Farm flour, but you can choose any plain/all-purpose gluten-free flour blend, provided it doesn't stray too far from the typical blend noted above. King Arthur gluten-free multi-purpose flour and Bob's Red Mill gluten-free all-purpose baking flour are two recommended American brands that produce excellent baked goods.

Flour, teff

Teff flour is milled from the gluten-free teff grain. Typically used in ethiopia to make injera bread, I use it in small quantities in baking to add a wholegrain taste and texture as it produces quite a dense bake. Buy brown teff flour, as you can find a white version as well, and make sure that it is labelled as 'gluten-free'.

Milk, coconut

When coconut milk is recommended in a recipe, buy this in a can. It is a actually a mixture of coconut water and coconut cream, but it is thicker, more stable for cooking with and more flavourful than the dairy-free coconut milk alternatives that are now available in cartons in the milk chiller.

Milk, whole

Whole milk is required for baking. Don't try to substitute skimmed or semi-skimmed milk in recipes calling for whole milk as the differing fat contents will affect the bake. Particularly in the sponge cake recipes in this book, the butter content is lower than in a typical sponge and this is because a proportion of the fat is coming from the milk. The mixture will not become light and fluffy and your cakes will fail to rise properly.

Milk, almond
When a recipe calls for almond milk, be sure to use unsweetened almond milk as otherwise the end result will be too sweet.

Nuts and seeds
Nuts and seed should ideally be bought in small quantities and used as soon as possible after opening to ensure freshness. Once opened, I store mine in a Kilner jar in the fridge.

Oils
When adding oil to sweet bakes, use a neutral flavoured oil such as sunflower or vegetable. Oil is added to soften the texture and to help preserve the bakes for a little longer. If you don't have any oil when making a sponge cake, add in the same amount of extra butter instead.

When making savoury dishes, it is fine to use olive oil if that's your preference, but you can use any cooking oil.

Salt
A small amount of salt actually enhances the sweetness and flavours of bakes. Use fine-milled table or cooking salt rather than sea salt, unless the recipe specifically calls for that.

Spices
As with nuts and seeds, buy small quantities of spices. It may seem more expensive, but if you buy in bulk you run the risk of them going stale and having to throw them away. Wrap any open packets of spices in clingfilm/plastic wrap between uses, or make sure that their jars are sealed and store them in a cool, dry place.

Sugar, brown
Brown sugar is moist and adds a slight toffee/caramel flavour to bakes as well as a closer texture. Be sure to buy soft brown sugar, rather than demerara/turbinado, as this is a granulated brown sugar that won't incorporate into a mixture well.

Sugar, caster/granulated
Caster/granulated sugar is more finely milled that white sugar making it perfect for baking with. It will blend into a recipe seamlessly without leaving a gritty texture. It is also good for caramelizing on top of brûlées or making into caramel as the smaller particles dissolve faster and more evenly than white sugar.

Sugar, icing/confectioners'
Icing/confectioners' sugar is the most finely milled sugar of all. It is powdery and usually bright white, but you can find golden versions. Use it for making smooth frostings and for dusting over your bakes. If whisking up to make frostings, drape a kitchen cloth over the mixing bowl to avoid being enveloped in a sugar cloud!

Vanilla
Vanilla is called for in two forms throughout this book. As a pod/bean or as an extract.

When buying vanilla extract, try to find a high-quality product for maximum flavour. Although it is cheaper, avoid vanilla essence, which is a synthetic vanilla flavouring.

If you can't find vanilla pods/beans, a good alternative is to use vanilla bean paste, which is a thickened vanilla extract with the vanilla seeds suspended in it.

Xanthan gum
Xanthan gum is a really important ingredient in gluten-free baking. It is a natural product which acts as a binding ingredient, creating the bonds that gluten delivers when using wheat flour. This means that bakes will be soft and fluffy and pastry will be rollable.

It is only used in small amounts as a little goes a long way, and can be bought in small tubs from the free-from section of most supermarkets. Keep it dry, sealed and in a cool place between uses. Don't be tempted to add more than is specified in a recipe, as the texture will become too thick and may even end up being rubbery.

equipment and storage

If you are a seasoned baker, you will likely possess most of the necessary equipment for the recipes in this book. If new to baking I recommend investing in these pieces. Gluten-free bakes often lose their texture more quickly than non free-from bakes. Here are some general storage guidelines to help keep your bakes fresher for longer.

Essential equipment includes
Eelectronic weighing scales, a free-standing mixer or handheld electric whisk, a timer, wooden spoons, rubber spatulas, a whisk, a large metal spoon, a rolling pin, a set of measuring spoons, a chopping board, a good knife, jugs/pitchers, mixing bowls, a deep muffin pan, cake pans of varying sizes in pairs, 23-cm/9-inch tart and quiche pans and baking sheets.

Extras include
A food processor, a stick blender, a fine-mesh sieve/strainer, a palette knife, piping/pastry bags with various nozzles/tips, a pastry brush, 1-lb. (20 x 10 x 7.5-cm/8 x 4 x 3-inch) and 2-lb. (23 x 12.5 x 7.5-cm/9 x 5 x 3-inch) deep loaf pans, a square cake pan, a Swiss/jelly roll pan, a sugar thermometer, a cupcake plunger, silicone baking sheets, an icing/confectioners' sugar dredger, a cake turntable and a chef's blow torch.

Airtight containers in the form of Tupperware™ and clingfilm/plastic wrap are your friends!
Wrap things really well in clingfilm/plastic wrap to prevent them from drying out, or if they are not practical to wrap, store in an airtight container.

Keep cakes out of the fridge
Unless a cake contains fresh cream, keep it at room temperature, ideally covererd with a glass cake dome. Putting a cake into the fridge will harden the texture and dry it out.

Freezing
Undressed sponge cakes can be frozen quite successfully, wrap really well in clingfilm/plastic wrap and put into a plastic food storage bag for extra protection. Freeze for up to 1 month.

Sterilize jars for preserves and sauces
Before filling a jar, be sure to sterilize it first, following the instructions given on page 4.

storage guidelines

BAKE	KEEP ME	FOR
Cupcakes and sponge cakes	Covered, at room temperature	Up to 3 days
Rich fruit cakes	Wrapped, in a cool dry place	Up to 2 months
Biscuits/cookies	In a Tupperware™	Up to a week
Scones	Covered, in a warm place	24 hours
Tarts	Covered, in the fridge	Up to a week
Desserts	Covered, in the fridge	Up to 3 days
Jam/jelly and curd	In sealed jars, in the fridge	6 months–1 year

basic techniques

Don't worry if you don't know all of the proper terminology when baking. I know that it can be off-putting to read a recipe calling for techniques that you haven't heard of, but the recipes in this book have been developed and written so as to be straightforward enough for a new baker to follow. Here's a run-down of some of the most common techniques called for throughout, so that you can feel prepared.

Beating

This is essentially just mixing. When eggs are called to be beaten, use a fork to break the yolks and mix thoroughly until the yolk and whites fully combine. When beating a cake batter or other mixtures, use a wooden spoon or a paddle attachment in a free-standing mixer to mix things together vigorously.

Blind baking

This refers to baking a pastry case before the filling is added. It is sometimes required when the filling itself doesn't require baking in the oven, or if the filling is wet, it will prevent the case from becoming soggy as it bakes. Once lined, the pastry case will need to be weighted down with baking beans to prevent the unfilled case from developing air pockets underneath and bubbling up. Be sure not to put the beans directly onto the raw pastry, but sit them on a layer of baking parchment to avoid them becoming baked into the pastry case.

Blitzing

The electronic processing of ingredients, be that with a food processor or stick blender.

Creaming

This is a technique in which butter and sugar are beaten together vigorously. The end result of creaming the two ingredients is that they will be combined, pale and fluffy. It makes the end bake light and airy and can be done by hand but more easily in a free-standing mixer or using a handheld electric whisk.

Folding

Folding ingredients together is a gentle way of mixing which preserves the air that has been incorporated into them up to that point from escaping. You will ideally need to use a large metal spoon for the job. Lift and turn the two sets of ingredients together, slowly and gently, turning the bowl with your free hand as you do so, until they are fully amalgamated.

Frosting

Frosting is both the name for the fluffy buttercream used for decorating cupcakes and the process of adorning the cupcakes with it. Frosting can be done by hand with a palette knife, or for a more professional finish, using a piping/pastry bag with a piping nozzle/tip.

Kneading

Kneading typically refers to the stretching of dough on a worksurface using your hands. When baking with gluten kneading helps to develop the gluten within the dough to create a strong texture, but when baking gluten-free recipes, it is a method used to complete a mixing process or to bring a dough up to the correct temperature for rolling out.

To successfully knead, place the dough you are working with onto a clean worksurface and use the heels of your hands to press down the dough and then bring it back together into a ball, turning and repeating until the dough is smooth and doesn't crumble when you apply pressure.

Piping

The act of using a piping/pastry bag to decorate cookies or cakes with icing or frosting.

Rolling out

You may be required to roll out a pastry or biscuit dough. The easiest way to do this for gluten-free doughs is to use two layers of clingfilm/plastic wrap, one underneath the dough and one over the top of it. Use a rolling pin (or a wine bottle if you don't have one) and press quite firmly down onto the dough through the top layer of clingfilm/plastic wrap, rolling firstly away from you with the rolling pin and then bringing it toward you. Rotate your rolling pin position so as to roll the dough out evenly in all directions and keep the pressure the same as you roll to ensure it is of even thickness.

Rubbing in

This can be done using a food processor, free-standing or handheld electric mixer, or even by hand, and refers to the mixing of flour and butter (and sometimes sugar) until the mixture resembles fine breadcrumbs. If using a processor or electric mixer, pulse the mixture so as to avoid over-mixing and creating a dough rather than breadcrumbs.

Sifting

This refers to passing an ingredient or mixture through a fine-mesh sieve/strainer. For the most part, I don't think that sitfting is essential for most ingredients in most recipes. If you are making a smooth glaze or drizzle and you have particularly lumpy icing/confectioners' sugar, sift it to remove the lumps before mixing it with the wet ingredients, but please don't feel that you must sift everything.

Whisking or whipping

This incorporates air into an ingredient or mixture and will either make it stiff and stable (cream) or light and fluffy (sabayon). Whisking can be done by hand with a balloon whisk but it is quite hard work. If you can, use a handheld electric mixer or free-standing mixer with the whisk attachments. Whisk carefully, as once you reach the desired consistency you need to turn the whisk off immediately. If you overwhisk cream, but only by a little, you can rescue it by adding a littleunwhipped cream to the mixture and stirring in until fully combined.

basic pastry

The trick to working with gluten-free pastry is forward planning, as temperature is key. Allowing the pastry to chill before bringing it back up to room temperature is essential to prevent it from flaking and cracking when you roll it out. Shortcrust is ideal for tarts and quiches, while hot water pastry rolls out really well for topping a pie and is pliable enough to shape into pasties and sausage rolls. The quantities for both recipes can easily be doubled for larger batches and any excess wrapped and stored in the fridge.

shortcrust pastry

Prep: 10 minutes | Chill: 2 hours | Difficulty: ●○○○○

BASIC

460 g/3 cups plain/all-purpose gluten-free flour

1 teaspoon xanthan gum

1 teaspoon salt

225 g/15 tablespoons unsalted butter, cubed

1 egg

MAKES 2 CASES

CHOCOLATE

400 g/2²/₃ cups plain/all-purpose gluten-free flour

60 g/¹/₂ cup cocoa powder

1 tablespoon icing/confectioners' sugar

1 teaspoon xanthan gum

225 g/15 tablespoons unsalted butter, cubed

1 egg

Using either the basic or chocolate quantities of ingredients, put the dry ingredients and cubed butter into a food processor and pulse until they reach a fine crumb consistency.

Pour in the egg and 1–2 teaspoons of water and mix until completely combined. The mixture will start to come together.

Use your hands, being sure to avoid the blade, to bring together the dough, then lightly knead on a lightly floured worksurface.

Put the pastry ball onto a piece of clingfilm/plastic wrap, press into a disc shape and chill in the fridge for at least 2 hours, until firm.

Notes To make the pastry by hand, put the dry ingredients into a large bowl and mix. Add the butter and rub in using your fingertips to fine crumbs. Make a well in the centre and add the egg and water and then mix well with a table knife, until the mixture starts to clump together. Bring together and knead, wrap and chill as above.

When rolling out, don't use too much flour, as this will dry it out – I advise instead rolling between two sheets of clingfilm/plastic wrap to prevent it sticking without the need for excess flouring.

hot water pastry

Prep: 10 minutes | Chill: 2 hours | Difficulty: ●○○○○

290 g/2 cups plain/all-purpose gluten-free flour

¹/₂ teaspoon xanthan gum

¹/₂ teaspoon salt

100 g/6¹/₂ tablespoons vegetable shortening, cubed (I use Trex)

1 egg

120 g/¹/₂ cup water, recently boiled

MAKES 1 BATCH

This is most easily done using a food processor. Put the dry ingredients and cubed vegetable shortening in and pulse to fine crumbs.

Pour in the egg, mix briefly and then, with the mixer still running, pour in the hot water slowly and mix until completely combined. The mixture will be a smooth and almost paste-like.

Use a metal spoon to scrape the mixture onto a piece of clingfilm/plastic wrap that has been lightly floured. Wrap the pastry in the clingfilm/plastic wrap and shape into a disc.

Chill in the fridge, for at least 3 hours, until completely cold and firmer to the touch.

Notes To make the pastry by hand, put the dry ingredients into a large bowl and mix. Add the vegetable shortening and, with a handheld electric whisk set to a low speed, mix to fine crumbs. Pour in the egg and mix briefly, then, with the mixer still running, pour in the hot water slowly and mix until completely combined. The mixture will be a smooth and almost paste-like and will stick to your blades quite a bit. Wrap and chill as above.

This pastry is very wet when first made, and requires chilling before it can be used. Don't worry that you seem to have made more of a paste than a pastry, just wrap it up and come back to it in a few hours and it will be perfect!

fillings and sauces

lemon curd

Not only does this homemade lemon curd taste absolutely delicious, it's also rather therapeutic to make. Don't worry if the curd takes a while to thicken, keep whisking and your patience will pay off.

Prep: 20 minutes | Cook: 15-20 minutes
Difficulty: ●●○○○

250 g/1¼ cups caster/granulated sugar

6 egg yolks

zest and juice of 4 large lemons

250 g/2 sticks chilled unsalted butter, cubed

sterilized glass jars with airtight lids

MAKES 2–3 JARS

In a large bowl set over a pan of simmering water, whisk together the sugar, egg yolks, lemon zest and juice until the sugar has dissolved.

Whisk in the butter, a few cubes at a time, allowing each addition to melt completely before adding the next.

Once all the butter is added, continue to whisk the mixture set over the pan until it thickens, which will take about 10 minutes. Be sure not to let the bowl touch the water or the mixture to overheat as this could cause it to curdle.

Remove the bowl from the heat, allow to cool slightly before pouring into sterilized jars to set.

Seal tightly with the lids and turn upside-down to cool – this will help to create an airtight seal in the jar. Once cool, store in the fridge for up to 1 year.

raspberry jam/jelly

This recipe is great for summer months when you can raid hedgerows for a glut of berries. Raspberries contain natural pectin so there's no need to use jam/jelly sugar, white sugar will do the job just fine.

Prep: 20 minutes | Cook: 15-20 minutes
Difficulty: ●●○○○

500 g/3½ cups fresh raspberries, rinsed and patted dry

500 g/2½ cups caster/granulated sugar

juice of ½ lemon

a sugar thermometer

sterilized glass jars with airtight lids

MAKES 2 JARS

In a large saucepan, heat the raspberries and sugar over a low heat until the sugar dissolves.

Increase the heat and bring to a rolling boil. Allow to boil, unstirred, for 5 minutes, then check the temperature using a sugar thermometer, which you want to be at 105°C (220°F).

Once the jam/jelly reaches setting point, remove from the heat and pour or ladle straight into sterilized jars to set.

Seal tightly with the lids and turn upside-down to cool – this will help to create an airtight seal in the jar. Once cool, store in the fridge for up to 1 year.

custard sauce

I'm definitely not knocking a good-quality store-bought custard sauce, but it is lovely to make your own for a special occasion, or to know how in case you suddenly find yourself caught short.

Prep: 10 minutes | Cook: 10–15 minutes
Difficulty: ●○○○○

4 egg yolks

2 tablespoons cornflour/cornstarch

75 g/$^1/_3$ cup caster/granulated sugar

seeds from 1 vanilla pod/bean

400 g/1$^2/_3$ cups double/heavy cream

400 g/1$^2/_3$ cups whole milk

SERVES 6–8

Whisk together the egg yolks, cornflour/cornstarch, sugar and vanilla in a jug/pitcher.

Heat the cream and milk together in a saucepan set over a low heat until just simmering, then pour over the egg yolk mixture.

Whisk and then pour back into the saucepan and return to a low heat. Cook for 5–10 minutes, stirring constantly, until thickened.

Serve immediately.

chocolate sauce

Perfect for pouring over ice cream, or serving with profiteroles, this is a silky smooth chocolate sauce that is best served warm, so make it just before you need it.

Prep: 10 minutes | Cook: 10 minutes
Difficulty: ●○○○○

100 g/3$^1/_2$ oz. dark/bittersweet chocolate, chopped

100 g/6$^1/_2$ tablespoons whole milk

100 g/6$^1/_2$ tablespoons double/heavy cream

20 g/1 tablespoon plus 1 teaspoon unsalted butter

20 g/2 tablespoons caster/granulated sugar

SERVES 4

Put the chocolate in a bowl and set aside.

Put all of the other ingredients into a saucepan and set over a low heat until the butter has melted and the sugar has dissolved. Bring to a simmer.

Pour over the chocolate in the bowl and whisk until the chocolate has melted and the sauce is smooth.

Serve immediately.

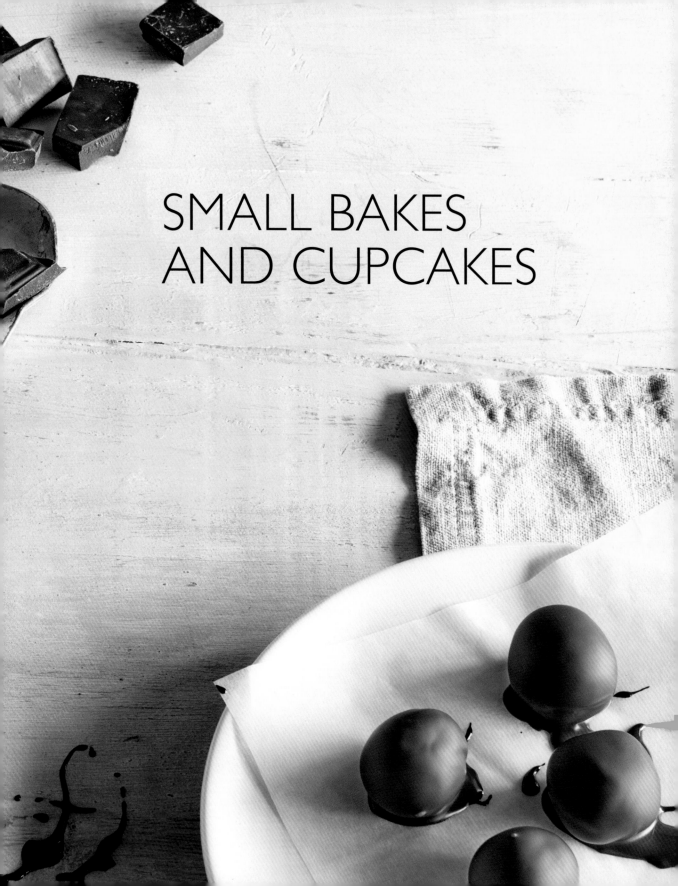

SMALL BAKES
AND CUPCAKES

These decadent brownies are one of our staple desserts at 2 Oxford Place. We serve them warm with ice cream or custard, and there's never a crumb left over. As a hardened chocoholic, I prefer my brownies unadulterated. But to ring the changes these are great with the addition of pecans, white chocolate chips, fresh raspberries or dried cranberries. Simply throw a handful or two into and onto the batter before baking.

From start to serve: 1 hour | Prep: 15 minutes | Bake: 25 minutes | Difficulty: ●○○○○

brownies

250 g/8 oz. dark/bittersweet chocolate, chips or chopped

125 g/1 stick unsalted butter

125 g/1 stick salted butter

5 eggs

175 g/³/4 cup plus 2 tablespoons soft light brown sugar

200 g/1 cup caster/granulated sugar

120 g/³/4 cup plus 1 tablespoon plain/all-purpose gluten-free flour

60 g/¹/2 cup cocoa powder

a large square baking pan greased and lined with baking parchment (about 38 x 28 cm/15 x 11 inches)

MAKES 12–16

Preheat the oven to 190°C (375°F) Gas 5.

In a jug/pitcher in bursts of 10 seconds in the microwave, or in a heatproof bowl set over a pan of simmering water, melt the chocolate and butters together. Stir to combine until molten and smooth, then cool slightly.

In a large bowl, or the bowl of a free-standing mixer, combine the eggs and both sugars. Whether using a handheld electric whisk, a free-standing mixer with the whisk attachment or whisking by hand, whisk up the eggs and sugar vigorously until thick and pale.

Tip the flour and cocoa powder into a large mixing bowl.

Once pale and thick, continue to mix the eggs on a slow speed and pour in the melted chocolate and butter mixture. When these are fully combined, stop whisking and add the flour and cocoa mixture. (You need to stop the whisk at this stage to avoid a flour shower.)

Whisk again, beginning slowly and briefly increasing the speed once combined. Within a minute there should be no lumps remaining and you'll have a thick, glossy, chocolatey batter.

Pour the batter into the prepared baking pan and level with a spoon or spatula. Bake in the preheated oven for 25 minutes, checking after 20, until risen with a papery crust. The top of the brownie may crack, but don't worry, it will sink back together on cooling.

Remove the pan from the oven and gently shake the brownie or press the top with your finger. It should feel almost set, but with a slight wobble.

Set the pan on a wire rack and cool for as long as you can resist before portioning into 16 sensible or 12 generous pieces. (This brownie portions like a dream if placed in the fridge for a couple of hours first.)

Enjoy right away or store in an airtight container in the fridge for up to 1 week and warm up before serving.

This recipe idea was met with some scepticism when it was first tentatively floated. My mum, a traditional scone aficionado, certainly raised an eyebrow. Cut to an hour later and the look of delight as we devoured the products of a trial batch, still warm from the oven, with oozing melted chocolate chips.

From start to serve: 50 minutes | Prep: 15 minutes | Bake: 20 minutes | Difficulty: ●●○○○

double chocolate scones

200 g/1^1/$_3$ cups plain/all-purpose gluten-free flour, plus extra for dusting

25 g/3 tablespoons cocoa powder, plus extra for dusting

40 g/3 tablespoons caster/granulated sugar

18 g/4^1/$_2$ teaspoons baking powder

a pinch of salt

^{1}/$_4$ teaspoon xanthan gum

40 g/3 tablespoons salted butter, softened

150 ml/^{2}/$_3$ cup buttermilk

1 egg

100 g/^{2}/$_3$ cup chocolate chips (dark/bittersweet, milk/semi-sweet or white)

clotted cream, to serve

a straight-edged square cookie cutter (2–3 cm/1–1^1/$_4$ inches)

1–2 baking sheets lined with baking parchment or silicone baking mats

MAKES 4–6

Preheat the oven to 190°C (375°F) Gas 5.

To a large bowl, or the bowl of a free-standing mixer, add the flour, cocoa powder, sugar, baking powder, salt and xanthan gum. Add the softened butter to the dry ingredients in small pieces. Either rub in by hand or on a slow speed in a mixer until the mixture resembles breadcrumbs.

In a jug/pitcher, combine the buttermilk and egg, then pour into the dry mixture. Stir together using a large metal spoon or again on a slow speed if using a mixer. Once you have a sticky dough, stop mixing. At this point, quickly stir in the chocolate chips until evenly distributed.

Dust the work surface well with a mixture of flour and cocoa powder and tip the dough onto it. Using your hands, briefly knead the dough, then gently press into a flat disc approximately 2–3-cm/1–1^1/$_4$-inches deep.

Stamp out scones from the dough using the straight-edged cookie cutter. Push straight down and lift the cutter straight up, as twisting will prevent the scones from rising evenly in the oven. Bring together the remaining dough and re-knead briefly, then stamp out more scones.

Arrange the scones on the prepared baking sheets. Space them out to allow for spreading and rising.

Bake in the preheated oven for 15–20 minutes until risen, golden and firm to the touch. You can check the scones are done by carefully lifting and tapping the bottom – they should make a hollow sound.

Cool the scones on a wire rack before serving with clotted cream.

Note These are fabulous eaten on their own, when still warm and the chocolate chips are melted. You can also try them with butter or chocolate-hazelnut spread. I recommend eating them on the same day as baking. If you are keeping them overnight, warm them for a few minutes in the oven before serving.

Variation For a quirkier take, add in a little grated orange zest and substitute chopped orange-flavoured chocolate for the chocolate chips.

Scones, the ultimate tea-time treat and as British a bake as can be. These were one of the trickiest recipes to master in gluten-free form, but hopefully you'll agree that this recipe cracks it. If you are used to baking scones, you'll notice I've upped the amount of liquid compared to a traditional recipe – gluten-free flour absorbs more liquid than wheat flour, so this is needed to compensate and give you the perfect rise and fluffy crumb.

From start to serve: 50 minutes | Prep: 15 minutes | Bake: 20 minutes | Difficulty: ●●○○○

classic scones

225 g/1^1/$_2$ cups plain/all-purpose gluten-free flour, plus extra for dusting

40 g/3 tablespoons caster/granulated sugar

18 g/4^1/$_2$ teaspoons baking powder

a pinch of salt

^{1}/$_4$ teaspoon xanthan gum

40 g/3 tablespoons salted butter, softened

140 ml/^{1}/$_2$ cup plus 1^1/$_2$ tablespoons buttermilk

1 egg

75 g/^{1}/$_2$ cup sultanas/golden raisins

1 beaten egg, to glaze

butter, jam/jelly and clotted cream, to serve

a straight-edged round cookie cutter (5–6 cm/2–2^1/$_2$ inches diameter)

1–2 baking sheets lined with baking parchment or silicone baking mats

MAKES 4–6

Preheat the oven to 190°C (375°F) Gas 5.

To a large bowl, or the bowl of a free-standing mixer, add the flour, sugar, baking powder, salt and xanthan gum. Add the softened butter to the dry ingredients in small pieces. Either rub in by hand or on a slow speed in a mixer until the mixture resembles breadcrumbs.

In a jug/pitcher, combine the buttermilk and egg, then pour into the dry mixture. Stir together using a large metal spoon or again on a slow speed if using a mixer. Once you have a sticky dough, stop mixing. At this point, quickly stir in the sultanas/golden raisins until evenly distributed.

Dust the work surface well with flour and tip the dough onto it. Using your hands, briefly knead the dough, then gently press into a flat disc approximately 2–3-cm/1–1^1/$_4$-inches deep.

Stamp out scones from the dough using the straight-edged cookie cutter. Push straight down and lift the cutter straight up, as twisting will prevent the scones from rising evenly in the oven. Bring together the remaining dough and re-knead briefly, then stamp out more scones.

Arrange the scones on the prepared baking sheets. Space them out to allow for spreading and rising. Brush the tops with the beaten egg to glaze, then bake in the preheated oven for 15–20 minutes until risen, golden and firm to the touch. You can check the scones are done by carefully lifting and tapping the bottom – they should make a hollow sound.

Cool the scones on a wire rack before serving – with butter, jam/jelly and clotted cream, of course!

Note Scones are always best served as fresh as possible. I recommend eating them on the same day as baking. If you are keeping them overnight, warm them for a few minutes in the oven before serving.

Variations If you prefer your scones plain, simply omit the sultanas/golden raisins. Or swap in the same quantity of dried cranberries or chopped dried apricots, or the zest of 1 lemon and 1–2 tablespoons poppy seeds.

A shortbread biscuit base beneath a layer of luscious caramel finished with a chocolate topping, this slice is something of a labour of love, given the required setting time in the fridge, but it is absolutely worth it. And remember, 'more haste, less speed' – don't be tempted to try and portion the shortbread until everything is completely set.

From start to serve: 3 hours | Prep: 20 minutes | Bake: 20-25 minutes | Difficulty: ●●○○○

millionaire's shortbread

SHORTBREAD

200 g/1^{1}/$_{3}$ cups plain/all-purpose gluten-free flour

50 g/^{1}/$_{4}$ cup caster/granulated sugar

a pinch of salt

100 g/6^{1}/$_{2}$ tablespoons unsalted butter, softened

^{1}/$_{2}$ tablespoon whole milk

CARAMEL

100 g/6^{1}/$_{2}$ tablespoons unsalted butter, in cubes

30 g/2^{1}/$_{2}$ tablespoons soft light brown sugar

a 397-g/14-oz. can sweetened condensed milk

20 g/1 tablespoon plus 1 teaspoon golden syrup/light corn syrup

2 tablespoons icing/confectioners' sugar

CHOCOLATE TOPPING

150 g/5 oz. dark/bittersweet chocolate

100 g/3^{1}/$_{2}$ oz. white chocolate

a 20-cm/8-inch square baking pan lined with baking parchment

MAKES 12–15

Preheat the oven to 190°C (375°F) Gas 5.

First make the shortbread. In a bowl, or using a food processor on pulse setting, rub together the flour, sugar, salt and butter until the mixture is in fine breadcrumbs. Stir in the milk, then tip the shortbread mixture into the prepared baking pan. Use the back of a spoon or your hands to press the mixture across the base of the tin, so that it is even and compact.

Bake in the preheated oven for 20–25 minutes until golden brown, then remove and set to one side.

To make the caramel, put the butter, sugar, condensed milk and syrup into a heavy-bottomed saucepan. Melt together over a low heat. Bring the caramel to a simmer, stirring continuously with a wooden spoon (this is very important, as otherwise the caramel will catch on the bottom of the pan and burn). Cook for 5–7 minutes, continuing to stir, until the mixture thickens and begins to darken.

Pour the caramel over the shortbread base, spreading with a spoon if necessary. Be careful not to touch the caramel at this stage as it will be extremely hot. Allow to cool completely.

When the caramel has cooled and is firm, melt the chocolates in separate bowls. Break each slab into pieces and either use the microwave to heat in bursts of 10 seconds or set the bowls over pans of simmering water. Both chocolates need to be melted at the same time.

Spoon the dark/bittersweet chocolate onto the caramel first, in evenly spaced spoonfuls and then between the dark/bittersweet chocolate, spoon the white chocolate. Use a table knife to swirl the two together so that all of the caramel is covered in an even layer.

Put the pan in the fridge for a few hours, then, once completely set, invert the pan onto a chopping board. Keep the shortbread upside down on the chopping board (as this helps prevent the chocolate from cracking too much when it is cut) and portion into 12–15 pieces using a sharp knife.

Serve chocolate-side up. Keeps in an airtight container for up to 1 week.

As a child, a brandy snap filled with whipped cream was a staple Sunday-afternoon treat. Serve these delicate, gingery biscuits in the same way, or with ice cream for dessert. Although they look impressive, there really is no magic involved in creating these delights. All it takes is a very watchful eye, the necessary tools to hand and a little practice. Prepare the mixture in advance, ideally the day before, but at least by 2–3 hours, so that it has a chance to firm up in the fridge before baking.

From start to serve: 3½ hours | Prep: 15 minutes | Bake: 30 minutes | Difficulty: ●●●○○

brandy snaps

50 g/3½ tablespoons unsalted butter

50 g/3 tablespoons golden syrup/light corn syrup

50 g/¼ cup soft light brown sugar

60 g/scant ½ cup plain/all-purpose gluten-free flour

½ teaspoon ground ginger

¼ teaspoon xanthan gum

a baking sheet lined with baking parchment or a silicone baking sheet

a rolling implement – a miniature rolling pin or a wooden spoon with a thick handle work nicely – oiled

MAKES 12–16

Melt the butter, golden syrup/light corn syrup and sugar in a pan over a low heat or a in 10-second bursts in the microwave. Stir together until the sugar is dissolved. Beat in the flour, ginger and xanthan gum using a wooden spoon or in a free-standing mixer with the paddle attachment until smooth. Transfer to a mixing bowl and allow to cool. Transfer to the fridge and chill completely until firm.

Preheat the oven to 190°C (375°F) Gas 5.

Take a heaped teaspoon of the chilled biscuit dough and roll into a ball. Repeat so you have four balls; place on the lined baking sheet, spaced well apart.

Bake in the preheated oven for 6–8 minutes. The mixture will flatten, become lace-like and darken to a caramel-brown colour.

Remove the baking sheet from the oven and place on a flat surface. Allow to cool for 1–2 minutes, then, using a palette knife, lift the edge of a disc to check if they are firm enough to lift and shape.

When the biscuit discs can be lifted without breaking, carefully roll one at a time around the oiled rolling pin or wooden-spoon handle. Press into position with the palm of your hand, overlapping the sides if possible. Allow to set for 30 seconds and then gently slide off and place on the work surface to cool completely.

Repeat the shaping process for the remaining 3 discs. If they become too cool and brittle to shape, return the baking sheet to the oven for 15–20 seconds to soften them back up.

Repeat the rolling, baking and shaping with the remaining mixture until it has all been used.

Alternatively, make just as many brandy snaps as you require and store the remaining dough in the fridge wrapped in clingfilm/plastic wrap for up to a fortnight, and bake at a later date.

I have to admit I came late to the rocky road party. It wasn't until working in a school where it was served as a dessert that I realized its enormous appeal. Teachers would grab as many pieces as possible and rush them up to the staff room for mid-afternoon marking slumps. The kids would eschew football to line up for seconds. And everybody would be debating what should or shouldn't be in a rocky road: cherries, sultanas/golden raisins, nuts? This is my standard version, but even I ring the changes regularly, so try one of the variations below. Oh, and as it's a no-bake recipe, it's perfect for little ones to help out with.

From start to serve: 4 hours | Prep: 15 minutes | Set: 3–4 hours | Difficulty: ●○○○○

rocky road

150 g/5 oz. dark/bittersweet chocolate, chopped

75 g/5 tablespoons unsalted butter, cubed

50 g/3 tablespoons golden syrup/light corn syrup

150 g/5 oz. gluten-free digestive biscuits/graham crackers

50 g/^{1}/3 cup blanched almonds, chopped

75 g/^{1}/2 cup glacé cherries, halved

100 g/2^1/2 cups mini marshmallows

icing/confectioners' sugar, for dusting (optional)

a 20-cm/8-inch square baking pan lined with baking parchment

MAKES 12–16

In a saucepan, gently melt together the chocolate, butter and golden syrup/light corn syrup until completely combined. Remove from the heat and set aside.

Break up the digestive biscuits/graham crackers into a rough rubble – you can chop them or put them in a plastic food bag, wrap in a kitchen cloth and bash with a rolling pin.

Put the biscuit bits into a large bowl and stir in the almonds, cherries and mini marshmallows.

Pour over the melted chocolate mixture and stir together with a large spoon or spatula until everything is well coated.

Tip the mixture into the prepared baking pan, spreading out and lightly pressing down.

Put the pan in the fridge and allow to set for 3–4 hours until firm.

Invert the pan onto a chopping board to remove the rocky road. Peel off the baking parchment, then slice into 12–16 pieces.

Dust with icing/confectioners' sugar before serving, if you like. Store in an airtight container for up to 1 week.

Variations To make things a bit more grown-up, it's great to swap the cherries for 50 g/^{1}/3 cup chopped crystallized ginger and add 75 g/^{2}/3 cup dark/bittersweet chocolate chunks, or at Christmas time you can throw in 50 g/^{1}/3 cup dried cranberries and the zest of 1 large orange.

These crunchy, vanilla biscuit rings topped with royal icing were my absolute favourite thing about parties as a child. They are quite fun to make, and would be a particular treat for any gluten-free children in the family, hosting or heading to a birthday party, as I've not yet seen a shop-bought version. It's not necessary to make these biscuits in a ring shape: you can use any shaped cutter you like and any colour icing to match as well. What about pumpkins for Halloween or hearts for St Valentine's Day?

From start to serve: 2 hours | Prep: 1 hour | Bake: 15 minutes | Difficulty: ●●●○○

party rings

250 g/1^2/$_3$ cups plain/all-purpose gluten-free flour, plus extra for dusting

25 g/3 tablespoons cornflour/cornstarch

100 g/^{1}/$_2$ cup caster/granulated sugar

175 g/1^1/$_2$ sticks unsalted butter, cubed

1 teaspoon vanilla extract

250 g/2^1/$_4$ cups royal icing/confectioners' sugar

pink, yellow and purple gel food colour

a 5-cm/2-inch diameter cookie cutter

a 2-cm/^{3}/$_4$-inch diameter cookie cutter

2 baking sheets lined with baking parchment or silicone baking sheets

4 disposable piping/pastry bags

MAKES 12–14

Preheat the oven to 180°C (350°F) Gas 4.

In a bowl, or using a food processor on pulse setting, rub together the flour, cornflour/cornstarch, sugar and butter until the mixture resembles fine breadcrumbs. Stir in the vanilla extract and 1 teaspoon of water, and bring the mixture together using your hands to form a dough. Knead lightly.

Dust the work surface with flour, roll out the mixture to a thickness of 5 mm/^{1}/$_4$ inch and stamp out rounds using the larger cookie cutter. Use the small cutter to stamp out the middle of each disc to form a ring and gently lift onto the prepared baking sheets. Prick the rings lightly with the tines of a fork and bake in the preheated oven for 10–15 minutes until lightly golden all over.

Remove from the oven and cool completely on the baking sheets. (If the holes have shrunk or the rings spread during baking you can re-cut them immediately after you remove them from the oven to neaten the shape using the same cutters, without moving them from the baking sheets.)

To make the glaze, slowly mix together the royal icing/confectioners' sugar with 2 tablespoons of water with a handheld electric whisk or in a free-standing mixer with the whisk attachment. Whisk for 5–8 minutes until the icing stands in shiny, stiff peaks.

Divide between to four small bowls and colour three of the bowls using a few drops of gel food colouring, leaving one white, and then put into separate piping/pastry bags. Snip the ends from the bags carefully so as to make a small hole, then pipe outlines around the edge of the biscuits using different colours on each. Allow to set for 10 minutes.

Fill in the biscuits using the same colour as the outline and then pipe in stripes of contrasting colours while the glaze is still wet and streak using a toothpick to create a feathered effect. Allow to set before serving.

Store in an airtight container for up to 3 days.

I find it quite disheartening to find you have baked a cake and then have a lot of wastage from levelling it, or that just doesn't get eaten. Cake truffles are a great way to use up that leftover cake. They make cute gifts and are lovely served alongside coffee. They can be made from any sponge, and use any frosting that you have to hand. The undipped balls can be stored in the freezer for up to a month and then pulled out and coated as and when you need them. If you decide to use white chocolate to coat the truffles, simply double dip once the first coat has set so you get a good, solid finish.

From start to serve: 2 hours | Prep: 20 minutes | Set: 1–2 hours | Difficulty: ●●●○○

cake truffles

250 g/8 oz. leftover sponge cake

2–3 tablespoons leftover frosting

300 g/10 oz. milk/semi-sweet or dark/bittersweet chocolate, roughly chopped

MAKES ABOUT 12

Break up your leftover cake and put into a food processor or into a large bowl. Pulse or rub with your fingertips until the mixture resembles rough breadcrumbs and no large lumps remain.

Add the leftover frosting a tablespoon at a time and mix to combine evenly with the cake crumbs. You are looking for the mixture to hold together and be mouldable, but not so wet as to be sticky in your hands.

Once you're happy with the consistency, roll the mixture into balls roughly 20–25 g/³⁄4 oz. in weight, or about the size of a walnut in its shell.

Arrange on a sheet of baking parchment or a silicone mat on a baking sheet and put in the freezer for at least 30 minutes to set.

When the balls are chilled, melt the chocolate either in 10-second bursts in the microwave or in a bowl set over a pan of simmering water.

Stir until completely smooth, then dip in the truffles one at a time until completely coated in chocolate. Tap to remove the excess and put back onto the parchment or silicone mat.

Once all the truffles are dipped, put them in the fridge for an hour or more to set before serving. Store in the fridge for up to 1 week. Alternatively, store uncoated in the freezer for up to 1 month.

Note It's a do-it-yourself tool, but the easiest implement I've found for coating cake truffles is a fork with the middle tines bent back so that there is a gap for the excess chocolate to drip through. Alternatively you can use a regular fork or a wooden skewer.

Florentines are not quite a traditional cookie, more a suspension of nuts and fruit in a crisp but ever-so-slightly chewy caramel. Swathe the underside of these discs in dark chocolate and you have yourself a very elegant addition to your cup of tea. As robust as they are pretty-looking (thanks to being set with both caramel and chocolate), once completely cooled, they can be easily packaged up in a cellophane bag, decorated with a ribbon and given as a gift. My mum, in particular, would thank you for them.

From start to serve: 1 hour | Prep: 10 minutes | Bake: 6–8 minutes | Difficulty: ●●○○○

florentines

30 g/2 tablespoons unsalted butter

75 g/$\frac{1}{3}$ cup soft light brown sugar

30 g/2$\frac{1}{2}$ tablespoons plain/all-purpose gluten-free flour

50 g/3 tablespoons double/heavy cream

75 g/$\frac{3}{4}$ cup flaked/slivered almonds

25 g/3 tablespoons chopped walnuts, almonds or hazelnuts

50 g/3 tablespoons mixed peel, chopped

75 g/$\frac{3}{4}$ cup glacé cherries, chopped

200 g/6$\frac{1}{2}$ oz. dark/bittersweet chocolate

2 baking sheets lined with baking parchment or silicone baking sheets

MAKES 12

Preheat the oven to 180°C (350°F) Gas 4.

In a saucepan set over a low heat, melt together the butter, sugar and flour.

Add the cream to the pan, a little at a time, stirring after each addition. The mixture should be smooth and caramel in colour when you remove it from the heat.

Stir in the almonds, chopped nuts, mixed peel and cherries until evenly distributed and everything is coated in the caramel.

Allow the mixture to rest for 5 minutes; this will allow it to cool slightly and prevent over-spreading in the oven.

Drop tablespoons of the mixture onto the prepared baking sheets, spaced well apart – they will spread to about 10 cm/4 inches in diameter. Flatten each mound slightly, then bake in the preheated oven for 6–8 minutes until golden all over and the edges begin to darken.

Remove from the oven. Using the tip of a spoon, gently push the lacy edges of the Florentines towards the centre to create a more circular shape. Be very careful not to touch them at this stage, as the sugar will be extremely hot.

Allow to cool completely on the baking sheets.

Once cool, melt the chocolate in a jug/pitcher in the microwave, or in a heatproof bowl set over a pan of simmering water. Stir to combine until molten and smooth and then coat the underside of each Florentine with a good layer of chocolate, setting upside down on a wire rack to cool.

As the chocolate begins to set, use a fork to create the traditional wavy pattern on the underside of each Florentine and then allow to harden completely before serving. Store in the fridge for up to 1 week.

A light and fluffy vanilla-sponge cupcake is essential in any baker's repertoire. The trick to mastering the gluten-free version is to adopt a new method of sponge-making, eschewing the traditional all-in-one approach. The batter will be looser than seasoned bakers are accustomed to and can be made dairy-free.

From start to serve: 1½ hours | Prep: 15 minutes | Bake: 18–20 minutes | Difficulty: ●●○○○

basic vanilla cupcakes

240 ml/1 cup whole milk or unsweetened dairy-free milk

15 ml/1 tablespoon sunflower oil

2 eggs

1 vanilla pod/bean or 2 teaspoons vanilla extract

260 g/1¾ cups plain/all-purpose gluten-free flour

14 g/3½ teaspoons baking powder

¼ teaspoon salt

³⁄₈ teaspoon xanthan gum

250 g/1¼ cups caster/granulated sugar

70 g/5 tablespoons unsalted butter or dairy-free spread, softened

VANILLA FROSTING

140 g/9 tablespoons unsalted butter or dairy-free spread, softened

500 g/4⅓ cups icing/confectioners' sugar

2–3 tablespoons whole milk or unsweetened dairy-free milk

½ teaspoon vanilla extract

a 12-hole muffin pan lined with greaseproof paper cases

a piping/pastry bag fitted with a large star nozzle/tip

MAKES 12

Preheat the oven to 190°C (375°F) Gas 5.

In a jug/pitcher, combine the milk, oil, eggs and vanilla extract, if using.

To a large bowl, or the bowl of a free-standing mixer, add the flour, baking powder, salt, xanthan gum, sugar and softened butter. If using a vanilla pod/bean, split it in half using the tip of a knife and then scrape the seed from each half using the flat edge of the blade and add these to the dry ingredients. (The pod/bean itself can be saved for making vanilla sugar – simply pop into an airtight container with caster/granulated sugar, leave for 2 weeks for the flavours to combine, then use in bakes.)

With a handheld electric whisk or in a free-standing mixer, slowly mix the dry ingredients and the butter until the mixture resembles fine breadcrumbs. Continue to mix on a slow speed and pour in the wet ingredients. Once combined, turn the speed to medium and mix for 3–5 minutes until the batter thickens.

Divide the mixture evenly between the paper cases; you want them to be around two-thirds full.

Bake in the preheated oven for 18–20 minutes until the cupcakes are risen, golden and spring back when pressed lightly on the top.

Remove from the oven and allow to cool for a few minutes before removing the cakes from the pan and allowing to cool completely on a wire rack.

While the cupcakes are cooking, make the vanilla frosting. Again using a handheld electric whisk or in a free-standing mixer, mix together the butter and icing/confectioners' sugar until no large lumps of butter remain.

Slowly add the milk and vanilla extract and as the mixture starts to come together, increase the mixing speed to high. Beat until smooth and soft and a pipeable consistency. Continue to beat for added fluffiness. (If the mixture seems too dry, add a little more milk. If it is too slack, add icing/confectioners' sugar a few tablespoons at a time.) Transfer the frosting into the piping/pastry bag and pipe in gorgeous swirls onto the tops of the cooled cupcakes. Serve immediately or store in an airtight container for up to 3 days.

Strawberries and cream are nice for dessert. Marry them together into a cupcake and they are sublime. These are so summery that I recommend serving them alongside a glass of Pimms. In front of the tennis, of course.

From start to serve: 1½ hours | Prep: 20 minutes | Bake: 18–20 minutes | Difficulty: ●●○○○

strawberries and cream cupcakes

240 g/1 cup whole milk

15 ml/1 tablespoon sunflower oil

2 eggs

260 g/1¾ cups plain/all-purpose gluten-free flour

14 g/3½ teaspoons baking powder

¼ teaspoon salt

⅜ teaspoon xanthan gum

250 g/1¼ cups caster/granulated sugar

70 g/5 tablespoons unsalted butter, softened

150 g/1 cup strawberries, hulled and quartered lengthways

TO FINISH

200 ml/1 scant cup double/heavy cream

2 tablespoons icing/confectioners' sugar

2 tablespoons cornflour/cornstarch

12 fresh strawberries, sliced

a 12-hole muffin pan lined with greaseproof paper cases

a piping/pastry bag fitted with a large nozzle/tip of your choosing

MAKES 12

Preheat the oven to 190°C (375°F) Gas 5.

In a jug/pitcher, combine the milk, oil and eggs.

To a large bowl, or the bowl of a free-standing mixer, add the flour, baking powder, salt, xanthan gum, sugar and softened butter.

Using a handheld electric whisk or in the free-standing mixer, slowly mix the dry ingredients and the butter until the mixture resembles fine breadcrumbs. Continue to mix on a slow speed and pour in the wet ingredients. Once combined, turn the speed to medium and mix for 3–5 minutes until the batter thickens.

Divide the mixture evenly between the cases – you want them to be just under two-thirds full.

Take three or four strawberry pieces per cupcake and push into the cupcake batter, evenly spaced apart. Ensure that they are standing upright, as this will mean there is a taste of strawberry in every bite and they won't sink to the bottom of the cupcakes.

Bake in the preheated oven for 18–20 minutes until they are risen, golden and spring back when pressed lightly on the top.

Remove from the oven and allow to cool for a few minutes before taking the cakes from the pan and allowing to cool completely on a wire rack.

Once the cupcakes have cooled, stabilize your cream by whisking together the double/heavy cream, icing/confectioners' sugar and cornflour/cornstarch. When the cream has reached soft, fluffy peaks and is just stiff enough to be piped, transfer to the piping/pastry bag.

Pipe luscious swirls of cream atop the cupcakes and, just before serving, garnish with sliced fresh strawberries.

Note Given that these are topped with fresh cream, they are best enjoyed on the day of baking. That being said, stabilizing the cream with a little cornflour/cornstarch and icing/confectioners' sugar prevents it from softening, so, if needs be, these cupcakes can be stored in the fridge overnight and eaten within 2 days.

Dressing up your cupcakes for spring with frosting nests and chocolate eggs is a lovely way to spend an afternoon, and they are brilliant for a spring fête or bake sale. You could even make the cake bases in advance and then get the kids involved for the decorating. Vary the base flavour as you wish – I recommend vanilla, but you can use any of the cupcakes found in the pages of this book.

From start to serve: 2 hours | Prep: 30 minutes | Bake: 18–20 minutes | Difficulty: ●●●○○

spring nest cupcakes

240 ml/1 cup whole milk

15 ml/1 tablespoon sunflower oil

2 eggs

1 teaspoon vanilla extract

260 g/1$\frac{3}{4}$ cups plain/all-purpose gluten-free flour

14 g/3$\frac{1}{2}$ tablespoons baking powder

$\frac{1}{4}$ teaspoon salt

$\frac{3}{8}$ teaspoon xanthan gum

250 g/1$\frac{1}{4}$ cups caster/granulated sugar

70 g/5 tablespoons unsalted butter, softened

36 mini chocolate eggs

CHOCOLATE FROSTING

140 g/9 tablespoons unsalted butter, softened

425 g/3$\frac{1}{2}$ cups icing/confectioners' sugar

75 g/$\frac{2}{3}$ cup cocoa powder

4–6 tablespoons whole milk

a 12-hole muffin pan lined with greaseproof paper cases

a piping/pastry bag fitted with a large grass-piping nozzle/tip

MAKES 12

Preheat the oven to 190°C (375°F) Gas 5.

In a jug/pitcher, combine the milk, oil, eggs and vanilla extract.

To a large bowl, or the bowl of a free-standing mixer, add the flour, baking powder, salt, xanthan gum, sugar, and softened butter.

Using a handheld electric whisk or a free-standing mixer, slowly mix the dry ingredients and the butter until the mixture resembles fine breadcrumbs. Continue to mix on a slow speed and pour in the wet ingredients. Once combined, turn the speed to medium and mix for 3–5 minutes until the batter thickens.

Divide the mixture evenly between the cases; you want them to be just under two-thirds full.

Bake in the preheated oven for 18–20 minutes until they are risen, golden and spring back when pressed lightly on the top.

Remove from the oven and allow to cool for a few minutes before taking the cakes from the pan and allowing to cool completely on a wire rack.

Now, or while the cupcakes are baking, make the chocolate frosting. With a handheld electric whisk or in a free-standing mixer, slowly mix together, the butter, icing/confectioners' sugar and cocoa powder until no large lumps remain. Slowly add the milk, and as the mixture starts to come together increase the mixing speed to high. Beat for a few minutes until smooth and soft. If the mixture seems too dry, add a little more milk. If it is too slack, add icing/confectioners' sugar a few tablespoons at a time.

Transfer the frosting to the piping/pastry bag and pipe in a circle on top of the cupcakes, leaving an indent in the centre. Nestle three mini chocolate eggs into the centre of each cupcake, and serve. Store in an airtight container for up to 3 days.

Note If you prefer, make a vanilla frosting by omitting the cocoa powder and using 500 g/4 cups of icing/confectioners' sugar. This can then be coloured in pretty pastel shades using gel food colouring, if desired.

These cupcakes are so easy to make, but are something of a showstopper thanks to their unusual floral flavour. Lavender, when in season, can be found either growing wild or in a florist's – be sure to rinse it first if using fresh. Dried lavender can be bought online – try herbalists, health-food shops or craft stores.

From start to serve: 3 hours | Prep: 20 minutes | Bake: 18–20 minutes | Difficulty: ●●●○○

lavender cupcakes

350 ml/1^1/$_2$ cups whole milk

4 tablespoons lavender flowers, fresh or dried, plus extra to garnish

15 ml/1 tablespoon sunflower oil

2 eggs

260 g/1^3/$_4$ cups plain/all-purpose gluten-free flour

14 g/3^1/$_2$ teaspoons baking powder

^{1}/$_4$ teaspoon salt

^{3}/$_8$ teaspoon xanthan gum

250 g/1^1/$_4$ cups caster/granulated sugar

70 g/5 tablespoons unsalted butter, softened

LAVENDER FROSTING

140 g/9 tablespoons unsalted butter, softened

500 g/4^1/$_3$ cups icing/confectioners' sugar

purple gel food colouring (optional)

a 12-hole muffin pan lined with greaseproof paper cases

a piping/pastry bag fitted with a flower nozzle/tip

MAKES 12

Begin by infusing the milk with lavender. Put the lavender and milk into a saucepan over a low heat. Bring to a simmer for a minute or two, then transfer to a jug/pitcher and cover with clingfilm/plastic wrap. Leave to cool completely and, once cooled, strain the milk using a fine-mesh sieve/strainer, pressing the lavender to extract the aroma before discarding.

Preheat the oven to 190°C (375°F) Gas 5.

In a jug/pitcher, combine 240 ml/1 cup of the lavender milk, oil and eggs.

To a large bowl, or the bowl of a free-standing mixer, add the flour, baking powder, salt, xanthan gum, sugar and softened butter.

Using a handheld electric whisk or a free-standing mixer, slowly mix the dry ingredients and the butter until they resemble fine breadcrumbs. Continue to mix on a slow speed and pour in the wet ingredients. Once combined, turn the speed to medium and mix for 3–5 minutes until the batter thickens. Divide the mixture evenly between the cases; you want them to be around two-thirds full.

Bake and cool the cupcakes following the instructions on page 41.

To make the lavender frosting, using a handheld electric whisk or free-standing mixer, slowly mix together the butter and icing/confectioners' sugar until no lumps of butter remain. Slowly add the remaining lavender-infused milk and as the mixture starts to come together, increase the speed to high. Beat for about 5 minutes until smooth, soft and fluffy. Add a few drops of purple gel food colouring, if using. If the mixture seems too dry, add a little more milk. If it is too slack, add icing/confectioners' sugar a tablespoon at a time.

Use a toothpick to streak the inside of the piping/pastry bag with lines of food colouring to create a dappled effect. Transfer the frosting to the bag and pipe in concentric circles. Serve immediately, garnished with fresh lavender, or store in an airtight container for up to 3 days.

Note For a special occasion, crystallize fresh lavender flowers to decorate by dipping them into a mixture of 1 egg white and 1 tablepoon of water, then dust with caster/superfine sugar, tapping to remove the excess. Dry overnight on a sheet of baking parchment.

The perfect bake for summer days. Zesty and light, with a tart hidden centre, these beauties are ideal for adults and kids alike – your baking prowess will be the toast of the afternoon. If you have the time, homemade Lemon Curd (see page 18) tastes delicious, and is also rather therapeutic to make. A jar from the shop will do the trick just fine but, as always, do double-check it's gluten-free.

From start to serve: 1½ hours | Prep: 20 minutes | Bake: 18–20 minutes | Difficulty: ●●○○○

lemon cupcakes

240 ml/1 cup whole milk

15 ml/1 tablespoon sunflower oil

2 eggs

260 g/1¾ cups plain/all-purpose gluten-free flour

14 g/3½ teaspoons baking powder

¼ teaspoon salt

⅜ teaspoon xanthan gum

250 g/1¼ cups caster/granulated sugar

zest of 1 lemon

70 g/5 tablespoons unsalted butter, softened

200 g/6½ oz. lemon curd

LEMON FROSTING

140 g/9 tablespoons unsalted butter, softened

500 g/4⅓ cups icing/confectioners' sugar

3–4 tablespoons freshly squeezed lemon juice

a 12-hole muffin pan lined with greaseproof paper cases

a piping/pastry bag fitted with a large nozzle/tip of your choosing

MAKES 12

Preheat the oven to 190°C (375°F) Gas 5.

In a jug/pitcher, combine the milk, oil and eggs.

To a large bowl, or the bowl of a free-standing mixer, add the flour, baking powder, salt, xanthan gum, sugar, lemon zest and softened butter. Using a handheld electric whisk or a free-standing mixer, slowly mix the ingredients until the mixture resembles fine breadcrumbs. Continue to mix on a slow speed and pour in the wet ingredients. Once combined, turn the speed to medium and mix for 3–5 minutes until the batter thickens.

Divide the mixture evenly between the cases; you want them to be around two-thirds full.

Bake and cool the cupcakes following the instructions on page 41.

Once cooled, make a hollow in each cake. You can do this with a sharp knife or with a cupcake plunger available from kitchenware shops. Be careful not to break through the bottom of the cake, and reserve the tops from the removed centre piece.

Fill the hollows with lemon curd, then place the lid back onto the cake to form a smooth top for decoration.

To make the lemon frosting, using a handheld electric whisk or free-standing mixer, slowly mix together the butter and icing/confectioners' sugar until no large lumps of butter remain. Slowly add the lemon juice and as the mixture starts to come together, increase the mixing speed to high. Beat for 5 minutes until smooth, soft and fluffy. If the mixture seems too dry, add more lemon juice. If it is too slack, add a little icing/confectioners' sugar. Transfer the frosting into a piping/pastry bag and adorn your cupcakes.

Store in an airtight container for up to 3 days.

I can do without getting caught in the rain, but these dairy-free cupcakes would probably make it worth it. They are extremely moist and summery and make a particularly great addition to a garden party or barbecue. If you need to, you can leave out the rum, and add a little extra coconut milk to the frosting instead.

From start to serve: 2 hours | Prep: 30 minutes | Bake: 18–20 minutes | Difficulty: ●●○○○

piña colada cupcakes

240 ml/1 cup full-fat coconut milk, from a shaken can

15 g/1 tablespoon sunflower oil

2 eggs

260 g/1¾ cups plain/ all-purpose gluten-free flour

14 g/3½ teaspoons baking powder

¼ teaspoon salt

⅜ teaspoon xanthan gum

250 g/1¼ cups caster/ granulated sugar

70 g/5 tablespoons dairy-free spread

120 g/4 oz. fresh pineapple, chopped into 1-cm/⅜-inch chunks, plus extra to decorate

dessicated/shredded coconut, to garnish

COCONUT FROSTING

120 g/8 tablespoons dairy-free spread

500 g/4⅓ cups icing/ confectioners' sugar

1–2 tablespoons white rum

1–2 tablespoons coconut milk

a 12-hole muffin pan lined with greaseproof paper cases

a piping/pastry bag fitted with a nozzle/tip of your choosing (optional)

SERVES 8–12

Preheat the oven to 190°C (375°F) Gas 5.

In a jug/pitcher, combine the coconut milk, oil and eggs.

To a large bowl, or the bowl of a free-standing mixer, add the flour, baking powder, salt, xanthan gum, sugar and dairy-free spread.

Using a handheld electric whisk or a free-standing mixer, slowly mix the dry ingredients and the dairy-free spread until the mixture resembles fine breadcrumbs. Continue to mix on a slow speed and pour in the wet ingredients. Once combined, turn the speed to medium and mix for 3–5 minutes until the batter thickens.

By hand, fold in the pineapple pieces, ensuring that you have drained them of any excess juice first.

Divide the mixture evenly between the cases; you want them to be just under two-thirds full.

Bake in the preheated oven for 18–20 minutes until they are risen, golden and spring back when pressed lightly on the top.

Remove from the oven and allow to cool for a few minutes before taking the cakes from the pan and cooling completely on a wire rack.

Now, or while the cupcakes are baking, make the coconut frosting. With a handheld electric whisk or free-standing mixer, slowly mix together the dairy-free spread and icing/confectioners' sugar until no large lumps remain. Slowly add the rum and coconut milk, a tablespoon of each at a time, and as the mixture starts to come together, increase the mixing speed to high. Beat until just smooth and soft, but be careful not to overbeat. If the mixture seems too dry, add a little more milk. If it is too slack, add icing/confectioners' sugar a few tablespoons at a time.

Transfer the frosting into the piping/pastry bag and pipe in swirls on top of the cupcakes. You can also use a palette knife to swirl the frosting on top, if you prefer. Sprinkle with dessicated/shredded coconut and decorate with sugared and charred pineapple chunks or a jaunty cocktail umbrella as a final flourish. Store in an airtight container for up to 2 days.

I am a sucker for an enormous swirl of frosting but, on occasion, even I acknowledge the beauty of a subtler approach. Enter the cherry bakewell cupcake – moist, almondy and enticing, there is no better topping to these than a simple slick of royal icing and a glacé cherry.

From start to serve: 2 hours | Prep: 30 minutes | Bake: 18–20 minutes | Difficulty: ●●●○○

cherry bakewell cupcakes

240 ml/1 cup whole milk

15 g/1 tablespoon sunflower oil

2 eggs

1/2 teaspoon almond extract

130 g/3 1/2 oz. marzipan, grated (see below)

260 g/1 3/4 cups plain/ all-purpose gluten-free flour

14 g/3 1/2 teaspoons baking powder

1/4 teaspoon salt

3/8 teaspoon xanthan gum

250 g/1 1/4 cups caster/ granulated sugar

70 g/5 tablespoons unsalted butter, softened

150 g/2/3 cup cherry jam/ jelly, to fill

250 g/2 1/4 cups royal icing/ confectioners' sugar

12 glacé cherries, to decorate

MARZIPAN

100 g/1/2 cup caster/ granulated sugar

100 g/1 scant cup icing/ confectioners' sugar

150 g/1 cup ground almonds

1 egg

1–2 teaspoons almond extract, to taste

a 12-hole muffin pan lined with greaseproof paper cases

If making your own marzipan, do so at least an hour in advance of baking the cupcakes. To a large bowl, or the bowl of a free-standing mixer, add the sugars and ground almonds. Add the egg and a quarter or half of the almond extract. Beat until everything comes together as a dough, adding a little extra icing/confectioners' sugar and ground almonds – a tablespoon at time of each, if the mixture seems too wet. Wrap in clingfilm/plastic wrap and chill in the fridge for at least 1 hour.

Preheat the oven to 190°C (375°F) Gas 5.

In a jug/pitcher, combine the milk, oil, eggs and almond extract.

Weigh out the marzipan and grate coarsely. The remainder can be stored in the fridge wrapped in clingfilm/plastic wrap.

To a large bowl, or the bowl of a free-standing mixer, add the flour, baking powder, salt, xanthan gum, sugar and softened butter. Using an electric handwhisk or a free-standing mixer, slowly mix the dry ingredients and the butter until they resemble fine breadcrumbs. Continue to mix on a slow speed and pour in the wet ingredients. Increase the speed and mix for 3–5 minutes until the batter thickens. Add the grated marzipan and mix until evenly distributed through the batter. Divide the mixture between the cases; you want them to be around two-thirds full. (You may find there's a little batter remaining, use to make a couple of extra cupcakes).

Bake and cool the cupcakes following the instructions on page 41.

Once cooled, carefully make a hollow in each cake, fill the hollows with a spoonful of cherry jam/jelly, then replace the sponge lid back on top.

Now make the royal icing. With an electric hand whisk or free-standing mixer, slowly mix together the royal icing sugar with 2 tablespoons of water. Whisk for 5–8 minutes until it stands in shiny, stiff peaks.

Use a spoon or palette knife to apply a smooth layer of royal icing to the cupcakes. Add a glacé cherry to the top of each and allow to set before serving. Store in an airtight container for up to 4 days.

MAKES 12

During the festive season it can be nice to ring the changes from traditional offerings. These are a fun adaptation of a Mince Pie (see page 102), with a very grown-up brandy buttercream topping. They are a marvellous way to use up any leftover mincemeat you find yourself with. Adding the mincemeat before baking the cakes means that these have a lovely hidden surprise in the centre.

From start to serve: 2 hours | Prep: 20 minutes | Bake: 18–20 minutes | Difficulty: ●●○○○

mince pie cupcakes

240 ml/1 cup whole milk

15 g/1 tablespoon sunflower oil

2 eggs

260 g/1²/₃ cups plain/all-purpose gluten-free flour

14 g/3¹/₂ teaspoons baking powder

¹/₄ teaspoon salt

1 teaspoon mixed spice/apple pie spice, plus extra to dust

³/₈ teaspoon xanthan gum

250 g/1¹/₄ cups soft light brown sugar

70 g/5 tablespoons unsalted butter, softened

200 g/1 cup mincemeat

BRANDY BUTTERCREAM

140 g/9 tablespoons unsalted butter, softened

500 g/4¹/₃ cups icing/confectioners' sugar

2–3 tablespoons brandy

2–3 tablespoons whole milk

a 12-hole muffin pan lined with greaseproof paper cases

a piping/pastry bag fitted with a large nozzle/tip of your choosing

MAKES 12

Preheat the oven to 190°C (375°F) Gas 5.

In a jug/pitcher, combine the milk, oil and eggs.

To a large bowl, or the bowl of a free-standing mixer, add the flour, baking powder, salt, mixed spice/apple pie spice, xanthan gum, sugar and softened butter. Using a handheld electric whisk or a free-standing mixer, slowly mix the dry ingredients and the butter to fine breadcrumbs. Continue to mix on a slow speed and pour in the wet ingredients. Once combined, turn the speed to medium and mix for 3–5 minutes until thick.

Divide the mixture evenly between the cases; you want them to be just under two-thirds full. You might have a little left over; use to make a few extra cakes. Add a teaspoon of mincemeat to the middle of each cupcake, on top of the cake batter. Be sure to add the mincemeat on top of the batter – it will sink slightly as the cakes bake and end up in the middle.

Bake in the preheated oven for 18–20 minutes until the cupcakes are risen, golden and the sponge springs back when pressed lightly. Be sure not to touch any visible mincemeat as it will be extremely hot. Remove from the oven, place the pan onto a wire rack and allow the cakes to cool completely before taking from the pan.

Now make the brandy buttercream. With a handheld electric whisk or free-standing mixer, slowly mix together the butter and icing/confectioners' sugar until no large lumps of butter remain. Add the brandy and milk, a tablespoon of each at a time, and as the mixture starts to come together, increase the mixing speed to high. Beat until smooth, soft and fluffy – about 5 minutes should do the trick. If the mixture seems too dry, add a little more brandy and milk. If it is too slack, add icing/confectioners' sugar.

Transfer the buttercream to the piping/pastry bag and pipe in swirls on the top of your cupcakes. Dust with mixed spice/apple pie spice and serve. Store in an airtight container for up to 3 days.

These are my absolute favourite cupcakes, both to bake and to eat. The lightness of the chocolate sponge perfectly tempers the richness of the filling and frosting and, dressed in gold cases, they are ideal for a cocktail party. For a glamorous touch of extra sparkle, dust the tops with edible gold shimmer powder.

From start to serve: 1½ hours | Prep: 20 minutes | Bake: 18–20 minutes | Difficulty: ●●○○○

chocolate hazelnut cupcakes

240 ml/1 cup whole milk

15 g/1 tablespoon sunflower oil

2 eggs

200 g/1⅓ cups plain/all-purpose gluten-free flour

60 g/½ cup cocoa powder

14 g/3½ teaspoons baking powder

¼ teaspoon salt

⅜ teaspoon xanthan gum

250 g/1¼ cups caster/granulated sugar

70 g/5 tablespoons unsalted butter, softened

200 g/1 scant cup chocolate hazelnut spread

75 g/½ cup chopped hazelnuts

CHOCOLATE FROSTING

140 g/9 tablespoons unsalted butter, softened

100 g/¾ cup plus 1 tablespoon cocoa powder

400 g/3½ cups icing/confectioners' sugar

4–6 tablespoons whole milk

a 12-hole muffin pan lined with greaseproof paper cases

a piping/pastry bag fitted with a large nozzle/tip of your choosing

MAKES 12

Preheat the oven to 190°C (375°F) Gas 5.

In a jug/pitcher, combine the milk, oil and eggs.

To a large bowl, or the bowl of a free-standing mixer, add the flour, cocoa powder, baking powder, salt, xanthan gum, sugar and softened butter. Using a handheld electric whisk or a free-standing mixer, slowly mix the dry ingredients and the butter until the mixture resembles fine breadcrumbs. Continue to mix on a slow speed and pour in the wet ingredients. Once combined, turn the speed to medium and mix for 3–5 minutes until the batter thickens.

Divide the mixture evenly between the cases; you want them to be around two-thirds full. (You may find there's a little batter remaining; use to make a couple of extra cupcakes.)

Bake and cool the cupcakes following the instructions on page 41.

Once cooled, make a hollow in each cake. Be careful not to break through the bottom of the cake and reserve the tops from the removed centres.

In a bowl, mix together the chocolate hazelnut spread and chopped hazelnuts, reserving 2 tablespoons of chopped nuts to decorate. Fill each hollow with a spoonful of the mixture and then place the cake pieces back onto the cakes.

Now, or while the cupcakes are baking, make the chocolate frosting. With a handheld electric whisk or free-standing mixer, slowly mix together the butter, cocoa powder and icing/confectioners' sugar until no large lumps of butter remain. Slowly add the milk and as the mixture starts to come together, increase the mixing speed to high. Beat for about 5 minutes until smooth, soft and fluffy. If the mixture seems too dry, add a little more milk. If it is too slack, add icing/confectioners' sugar a few tablespoons at a time.

Transfer the frosting to a piping/pastry bag fitted with a large nozzle of your choice and pipe swirls atop your cupcakes. Sprinkle with extra chopped hazelnuts and serve. Store in an airtight container for up to 3 days.

LARGER
CAKES

salted caramel cake

From start to serve: 4 hours | Prep: 20 minutes | Bake: 40–45 minutes | Difficulty: ●●●○○

360 ml/1^1/$_2$ cups whole milk

21 g/1^1/$_2$ tablespoons sunflower oil

1 teaspoon vanilla extract

3 eggs

390 g/2^2/$_3$ cups plain/all-purpose gluten-free flour

21 g/5^1/$_4$ teaspoons baking powder

^{1}/$_2$ teaspoon salt

^{1}/$_2$ teaspoon xanthan gum

275 g/1^1/$_3$ cups caster/granulated sugar, plus extra for creating shards

100 g/^{1}/$_2$ cup soft light brown sugar

105 g/7 tablespoons unsalted butter, softened

SALTED CARAMEL

200 g/1 cup caster/granulated sugar

100 g/6^1/$_2$ tablespoons unsalted butter, cubed

150 ml/^{2}/$_3$ cup double/heavy cream

1 teaspoon sea salt flakes

SALTED CARAMEL FROSTING

140 g/9 tablespoons unsalted butter, softened

2 tablespoons salted caramel

500 g/4^1/$_3$ cups icing/confectioners' sugar

1–2 tablespoons whole milk

2 x 20-cm/8-inch round cake pans greased and lined with baking parchment

a piping/pastry bag fitted with a large nozzle/tip

SERVES 12

Make the salted caramel at least 3 hours and up to 3 days in advance of baking the cakes, to allow it to cool down completely. Put the sugar in a large heavy-bottomed saucepan and whisk over a medium heat until completely melted. Cook, continuing to whisk, until the sugar has turned caramel in colour. Remove the pan from the heat, add the cubed butter and whisk until combined. Then slowly pour in the cream and whisk again. Finally add the salt, then set aside for 10 minutes before transferring to a bowl to cool completely. Store in the fridge if making well in advance.

Preheat the oven to 180°C (350°F) Gas 4. In a jug/pitcher, combine the milk, oil, vanilla extract and eggs.

To a large bowl, or the bowl of a free-standing mixer, add the flour, baking powder, salt, xanthan gum, sugars and softened butter. Using a handheld electric whisk or a free-standing mixer, slowly mix the dry ingredients and the butter until the mixture resembles fine breadcrumbs. Pour in the wet ingredients and continue to mix slowly. Once combined, turn the speed to medium and mix for 3–5 minutes until the batter thickens.

Divide the mixture evenly between the cake pans and level with a spoon. Bake the cakes in the preheated oven for 40–45 minutes until they are risen, golden and spring back when pressed lightly on the top – a skewer inserted into the centre of the cake should come out clean or crumbed. Put the pans onto wire racks to cool completely.

To make the salted caramel frosting, mix together the butter, salted caramel and icing/confectioners' sugar with a handheld electric mixer or in a free-standing mixer until no large lumps of butter remain. Use a slow speed to avoid an icing/confectioners' sugar cloud enveloping you and the kitchen. Slowly add the milk and as the mixture starts to come together, increase the mixing speed to high. Beat until smooth, soft and a pipeable consistency. Continue to beat for added fluffiness. (If the mixture seems too dry, add a little more milk. If it is too slack, add icing/confectioners' sugar a tablespoon at a time.) Transfer the frosting into the piping/pastry bag.

Once cooled, gently remove the cakes from the pans, loosening the edges with a table knife if necessary, and level. Place the first layer of sponge onto a serving plate or stand. Pipe a ring of frosting around the edge of the sponge, then fill with salted caramel. Add a sprinkle of extra sea salt flakes. Lay the second sponge on top and gently press down. Using a palette knife, lightly frost the top and sides of the cake and allow to set slightly.

Make decorative sugar shards following the method for spun sugar on page 86, pouring the caramel carefully onto an oiled sheet of foil to set before cracking. Warm up any remaining salted caramel and drizzle to over.

This celebration cake has wow-factor flavour and can be dressed up as elegantly as you like. If you are pushed for time, or want something simpler, omit the outer layer of frosting and dust with icing/confectioners' sugar instead.

Named for the vibrant hue of the sponge, this is a showstopper of a cake. Concealed beneath its coat of creamy white frosting, the first slice will deliver guaranteed oohs and aahs. This is a rich and dense sponge, which is not only delicious, but also makes the perfect base for decorating, shaping or stacking.

From start to serve: 3 hours | Prep: 25 minutes | Bake: 40–45 minutes | Difficulty: ●●●○○

red velvet cake

270 ml/1 cup plus 2 tablespoons buttermilk

15 g/1 tablespoon sunflower oil

3 eggs

3 teaspoons vanilla extract

1^1/$_2$ teaspoons cider vinegar

2 tablespoons red food colouring gel

300 g/2 cups plain/all-purpose gluten-free flour

30 g/^{1}/$_4$ cup cocoa powder

75 g/^{1}/$_2$ cup ground almonds

^{3}/$_4$ teaspoon bicarbonate of soda/baking soda

12 g/1 tablespoon baking powder

^{3}/$_4$ teaspoon salt

^{3}/$_4$ teaspoon xanthan gum

300 g/1^1/$_2$ cups caster/granulated sugar

135 g/9 tablespoons unsalted butter, softened

CREAM-CHEESE FROSTING

200 g/13 tablespoons unsalted butter, softened

500 g/4^1/$_3$ cups icing/confectioners' sugar

175 g/6 oz. full-fat cream cheese

2–3 x 20-cm/8-inch round cake pans, greased and lined with baking parchment

SERVES 12

Preheat the oven to 180°C (350°F) Gas 4.

In a jug/pitcher, combine the buttermilk, oil, eggs, vanilla, cider vinegar and red food colouring.

To a large bowl, or the bowl of a free-standing mixer, add the flour, cocoa powder, ground almonds, bicarbonate of soda/baking soda, baking powder, salt, xanthan gum, sugar and softened butter. With a handheld electric whisk or a free-standing mixer, slowly mix until the mixture resembles very fine breadcrumbs. Continue to mix on a slow speed and pour in the wet ingredients. Once combined, turn the speed to medium and mix for 3–5 minutes until the batter thickens.

Divide the mixture evenly between the cake pans and level with a spoon.

Bake in the preheated oven for 35–40 minutes if using three pans or 40–45 minutes if two. They are done when risen and spring back when pressed lightly on the top and a skewer inserted into the centre comes out clean.

Place the pans onto a wire rack and allow to cool completely. Once cooled, gently remove from the pans, loosening the edges with a table knife if necessary, carefully wrap the sponges in clingfilm/plastic wrap and put in the fridge for at least an hour.

Now make the cream-cheese frosting. Again using a handheld electric whisk or free-standing mixer, mix together the butter and icing/confectioners' sugar until no large lumps of butter remain. Use a slow speed to avoid a sugar cloud enveloping you and the kitchen. Add the cream cheese and as the mixture starts to come together, increase the mixing speed to high. Beat until just smooth, soft and fluffy, about 2–3 minutes but not for too long as the frosting could separate. If the mixture seems too dry, add a little more cream cheese. If it is too slack, add icing/confectioners' sugar a few tablespoons at a time.

Remove and unwrap the sponges. Level the tops with a serrated knife and place the first layer of sponge onto a serving plate or stand and top with a layer of frosting. Repeat with the second sponge, and third if you have it, and then envelop the entire cake in frosting.

A good carrot cake is essential ammunition in any baker's arsenal. It can be spruced up with cream-cheese frosting for special occasions, drizzled with orange glaze to keep it dairy-free or left naked for easy transportation on picnics. It's a doddle to make, with only very slight exertion required in the form of grating carrots. This recipe contains both nuts and sultanas/golden raisins, but will work without them, if that's your preference. It's also worth noting that should you find yourself with a glut of parsnips, simply substitute these for the carrots – the result will be different, but every bit as tasty.

From start to serve: 3 hours | Prep: 20 minutes | Bake: 45–55 minutes | Difficulty: ●●○○○

carrot cake

240 g/1¹⁄₄ cups soft light brown sugar

240 ml/1 cup sunflower oil

4 eggs

270 g/1³⁄₄ cups plain/all-purpose gluten-free flour

12 g/1 tablespoon baking powder

¹⁄₂ teaspoon xanthan gum

¹⁄₂ teaspoon salt

1 teaspoon bicarbonate of soda/baking soda

2 teaspoons mixed spice/apple pie spice

200 g/1 medium carrot, grated

zest of 1 orange

100 g/²⁄₃ cup sultanas/golden raisins

75 g/¹⁄₂ cup pecan nuts, chopped

ORANGE GLAZE
150 g/1¹⁄₃ cups icing/confectioners' sugar

3–5 tablespoons freshly squeezed orange juice

a 20-cm/8-inch square cake pan greased and lined with baking parchment

SERVES 12

Preheat the oven to 170°C (325°F) Gas 3.

To a large bowl, or the bowl of a free-standing mixer, add the sugar, oil and eggs. Whisk on a medium-high speed until thickened and slightly pale.

Add the flour, baking powder, xanthan gum, salt, bicarbonate of soda/baking soda and mixed spice/apple pie spice to the bowl and whisk again until you have a smooth, thick batter. Add the grated carrot, orange zest, sultanas/golden raisins and pecan nuts, and stir in until well combined.

Spoon or pour the mixture into the cake pan and bake in the preheated oven for 45–55 minutes, checking the cake after 45 minutes. The cake is done when risen and springs back when pressed lightly on the top – a skewer inserted into the centre of the cake should come out without any wet batter clinging to it.

Place the pan onto a wire rack and allow the cake to cool completely. Once cooled, gently remove from the pan, loosening the edges with a table knife if necessary.

At this stage the cake can be dusted with icing/confectioners' sugar and served just as it is. Alternatively, you can decorate with Cream-Cheese Frosting (see page 63).

For a dairy-free adornment, as pictured, prepare the orange glaze. Sift the icing/confectioners' sugar into a bowl. Stir in the orange juice a tablespoon at a time and mix well to form a viscous paste. Drizzle over the cake and allow to set before serving.

360 ml/1 1/2 cups whole milk

21 g/1 1/2 tablespoons sunflower oil

1 teaspoon vanilla extract

3 eggs

390 g/2 2/3 cups plain/all-purpose gluten-free flour

21 g/5 1/4 teaspoons baking powder

1/2 teaspoon salt

1/2 teaspoon xanthan gum

275 g/1 1/4 cups caster/granulated sugar

100 g/1/2 cup soft light brown sugar

105 g/7 tablespoons unsalted butter, softened

125 g/1 scant cup milk/semi-sweet chocolate chips

COOKIE DOUGH

60 g/4 tablespoons unsalted butter, softened

60 g/5 tablespoons soft light brown sugar

120 ml/1/2 cup sweetened condensed milk

125 g/1 cup plain/all-purpose gluten-free flour

1/4 teaspoon xanthan gum

1/4 teaspoon salt

100 g/2/3 cup milk/semi-sweet chocolate chips

BROWN-SUGAR FROSTING

175 g/1 1/2 sticks unsalted butter, softened

150 g/3/4 cup soft light brown sugar

300 g/2 1/2 cups icing/confectioners' sugar

2–3 tablespoons whole milk

3 x 20-cm/8-inch round cake pans greased and lined with baking parchment

SERVES 12

Cookie dough has to be one of life's greatest indulgences and this cake is an ode to it, with layers of chocolate-chip sponge and a brown-sugar frosting mirroring the star of the show.

From start to serve: 3 hours | Prep: 30 minutes | Bake: 40–45 minutes
Difficulty: ●●●○○

cookie dough cake

Preheat the oven to 180°C (350°F) Gas 4.

In a jug/pitcher, combine the milk, oil, vanilla extract and eggs.

To a large bowl, or the bowl of a free-standing mixer, add the flour, baking powder, salt, xanthan gum, sugars and softened butter. Using a handheld electric whisk or a free-standing mixer, slowly mix the dry ingredients and the butter until the mixture resembles fine breadcrumbs. Pour in the wet ingredients and continue to mix slowly. Once combined, turn the speed to medium and mix for 3–5 minutes until the batter thickens. Fold in the chocolate chips and then divide the mixture evenly between the cake pans and level.

Bake the cakes in the preheated oven for 40–45 minutes until they are risen and spring back when pressed lightly on the top. Put the pans onto a wire rack to cool completely. Once cooled, gently remove from the pans, loosening the edges with a table knife if necessary, and level.

While the cakes bake, make the cookie dough. Beat together the butter and sugar until fluffy. Add the condensed milk, flour, xanthan gum and salt, and beat again until smooth and well combined. Add the chocolate chips and mix in. Chill the cookie dough wrapped in clingfilm/plastic wrap in the fridge until you are ready to assemble the cake.

To make the brown-sugar frosting, with a handheld electric whisk or free-standing mixer, cream together the butter and brown sugar. Add the icing/confectioners' sugar and milk, and mix on a slow speed until no large lumps remain. As the mixture starts to come together, increase the mixing speed to high and beat for a few minutes until smooth and soft. If the mixture seems too dry, add a little more milk. If it is too slack, add icing/confectioners' sugar a few tablespoons at a time.

To assemble the cake, place the first layer of sponge onto a serving plate or stand. Roll out the cookie dough into a disc the same size as the sponge bases and place on top of the first layer of sponge, followed by the second sponge, then repeat. Using a palette knife, frost the tops and sides of the cake using the brown-sugar frosting and allow to set slightly before serving. Adorn with any kind of confectionery you have to hand – I like the combination of salted pretzels with broken cookies and melted chocolate.

Loaf cakes are lovely to have around. They slice well and their smaller size and simplicity means they are the perfect option for those 'just because' days when a bake seems essential, but there's no particular celebration in the offing. If you don't like poppy seeds, or don't have them to hand, you can leave them out.

From start to serve: 2½ hours | Prep: 20 minutes | Bake: 40-45 minutes | Difficulty: ●●○○○

lemon poppy seed drizzle loaf

240 ml/1 cup whole milk

15 g/1 tablespoon sunflower oil

2 eggs

260 g/1¾ cups plain/all-purpose gluten-free flour

14 g/3½ teaspoons baking powder

¼ teaspoon salt

⅜ teaspoon xanthan gum

250 g/1¼ cups caster/granulated sugar

zest of 2 lemons

70 g/5 tablespoons unsalted butter, softened

2 tablespoons poppy seeds

crème fraîche, to serve

GLAZE

freshly squeezed juice of 2 lemons

100 g/½ cup caster/granulated sugar

a 900-g/2-lb. loaf pan, greased and lined with baking parchment

SERVES 8–10

Preheat the oven to 180°C (350°F) Gas 4.

In a jug/pitcher, combine the milk, oil and eggs.

To a large bowl, or the bowl of a free-standing mixer, add the flour, baking powder, salt, xanthan gum, sugar, lemon zest and softened butter.

Whether using a handheld electric whisk or a free-standing mixer, slowly mix the dry ingredients and the butter until the mixture resembles fine breadcrumbs. Continue to mix on a slow speed and pour in the wet ingredients. Once combined, turn the speed to medium and mix for 3–5 minutes until the batter thickens. Add the poppy seeds and mix until evenly distributed.

Pour or spoon the batter into the loaf pan and level with the back of a spatula or spoon.

Bake in the preheated oven for 40–45 minutes until it is risen, golden and springs back when pressed lightly on the top. Remove from the oven and check that it is baked by inserting a clean skewer into the centre of the cake. It should come out clean or crumbed but without any wet batter clinging to it.

Put the pan onto a wire rack and allow to rest for 1–2 minutes while you mix together the glaze.

Stir together the lemon juice and in a bowl.

Without removing the cake from the pan, prick the surface all over with a fork or skewer and then pour over the glaze – it's important to do this while the cake is still warm. Leave the cake to cool completely in the pan on the wire rack, by which the time the glaze will have crystallized and set.

Remove the loaf from the pan, loosening the edges with a palette or table knife if necessary. Slice and serve – perhaps with a dollop of crème fraîche.

You can ring the changes with other citrus fruits – an orange or lime version is just as delicious.

I adore this cake, and not only because we share a moniker. It is simple but stunning, and the combination of textures and flavours just works. It might be traditional, but if it ain't broke...

From start to serve: 2 hours | Prep: 15 minutes | Bake: 40–45 minutes | Difficulty: ●●○○○

victoria sponge cake

360 ml/1^{1}/$_{2}$ cups whole milk

21 g/1^{1}/$_{2}$ tablespoons sunflower oil

1 teaspoon vanilla extract

3 eggs

390 g/2^{2}/$_{3}$ cups plain/all-purpose gluten-free flour

21 g/5 teaspoons baking powder

^{1}/$_{2}$ teaspoon salt

^{1}/$_{2}$ teaspoon xanthan gum

375 g/1^{3}/$_{4}$ cups plus 2 tablespoons caster/granulated sugar

105 g/7 tablespoons unsalted butter, softened

FILLING

150 ml/^{2}/$_{3}$ cup double/heavy cream

1 tablespoon icing/confectioners' sugar, plus extra for dusting

2 tablespoons cornflour/cornstarch

100 g/scant ^{1}/$_{2}$ cup strawberry jam/jelly

caster/granulated sugar, for dusting (optional)

2 x 20-cm/8-inch round cake pans, greased and lined with baking parchment

SERVES 12

Preheat the oven to 180°C (350°F) Gas 4.

In a jug/pitcher, combine the milk, oil, vanilla extract and eggs.

To a large bowl, or the bowl of a free-standing mixer, add the flour, baking powder, salt, xanthan gum, sugar and softened butter. Whether using a handheld electric whisk or a free-standing mixer, slowly mix until the mixture resembles fine breadcrumbs.

Continue to mix on a slow speed and pour in the wet ingredients. Once combined, turn the speed to medium and mix for 3–5 minutes until the batter thickens. Divide the mixture evenly between the pans and level with a spoon or spatula.

Bake the cakes in the preheated oven for 40–45 minutes until they are risen, golden and spring back when pressed lightly on the top.

Remove from the oven and check that the cakes are baked by inserting a clean skewer into the centre of each cake. It should come out clean or crumbed but without any wet batter clinging to it.

Put the pans onto a wire rack and allow to cool completely.

Once cooled, gently remove from the pans, loosening the edges with a table knife if necessary, and level the bottom layer if required.

Stabilize the cream for the filling by whisking together the double/heavy cream, icing/confectioners' sugar and cornflour/cornstarch. Watch the cream like a hawk as it whisks; it can quickly become overworked. You are aiming for fluffy peaks that are just stiff enough to support the top cake layer when assembled.

Place the first layer of sponge onto a serving plate or stand and top with strawberry jam/jelly.

Follow with a generous layer of whipped cream.

Place the top layer of sponge on top and generously dust with icing/confectioners' sugar, or caster/granulated sugar for a more traditional finish. Serve in slices.

If you can, make this traditional celebration cake in advance, ideally at least a fortnight and up to 3 months before Christmas, and feed it with brandy. By the time the big day comes, it will be moist and fruity and all ready for its marzipan and fondant party dress. A tot of sherry for the cook is also encouraged.

From start to serve: 24 hours | Prep: 25 minutes | Bake: 2½–3 hours | Difficulty: ●●○○○

christmas cake

750 g/1½ lbs. (about 5 cups) mixed dried fruit (currants, sultanas/golden raisins, dark raisins)

100 g/¾ cup chopped mixed peel

100 g/¾ cup glacé cherries

150 ml/⅔ cup brandy

250 g/2 sticks salted butter, softened

250 g/1¼ cups dark brown soft sugar

2 tablespoons black treacle/molasses

4 eggs

250 g/1⅔ cups plain/all-purpose gluten-free flour

½ teaspoon xanthan gum

2 teaspoons mixed spice/apple pie spice

brandy, to feed

a 23-cm/9-inch springform round cake pan, greased and lined with a double layer of baking parchment

SERVES 12–16

Put the dried fruit, peel and glacé cherries into a large mixing bowl. Gently warm the brandy, then pour over the fruit. Cover the bowl with clingfilm/plastic wrap and allow to sit for a minimum of 2 hours and up to 2 days in a cool, dark place.

Preheat the oven to 150°C (300°F) Gas 2.

In a large bowl, or the bowl of a free-standing mixer, cream the butter, sugar and treacle/molasses together. Add the eggs, flour, xanthan gum and mixed spice/apple pie spice to the bowl and beat again until combined. Add the soaked fruits with any remaining brandy and fold in using a large spoon or spatula.

Transfer the mixture into the prepared cake pan and level with a spoon or spatula.

Bake in the preheated oven for 2½–3 hours until a skewer inserted into the centre of the cake comes out clean or crumbed but without any wet batter clinging to it. Check the cake after 2 hours, and every 15 minutes thereafter. Cover with foil if the top is browning too much at any point.

When cooked, put the pan onto a wire rack and brush with a tablespoon or two more brandy. Allow to cool completely.

Once cooled, gently remove from the pan, wrap in a triple layer of baking parchment, foil and clingfilm/plastic wrap. Unwrap once a week and 'feed' the cake by brushing with a couple of tablespoons of brandy.

This fruit cake can be served plain (it's wonderful served with cheese and fresh figs), or can be decorated with marzipan and fondant icing fixed with jam/jelly.

Easy enough to whip up, the labour here is in keeping a semi-watchful eye over the pudding as it steams. Come Christmas, you will be the heralded as the ultimate host for preparing your own from scratch. It's not essential to hide a coin in the pudding, nor does it have to be doused with brandy and flamed at the table, but both are rather fun traditions, and I couldn't do without either.

From start to serve: 30 hours | Prep: 20 minutes | Steam: 5 hours | Difficulty: ●●●○○

christmas pudding

200 g/1^1/$_3$ cups sultanas/golden raisins

150 g/1 cup dark raisins

50 g/^{1}/$_3$ cup dried Zante currants

50 g/^{1}/$_3$ cup mixed peel

50 g/^{1}/$_3$ cup glacé cherries

100 ml/6^1/$_2$ tablespoons brandy

3 eggs

175 g/^{3}/$_4$ cup plus 2 tablespoons soft light brown sugar

80 g/^{2}/$_3$ cup plus 1 tablespoon plain/all-purpose gluten-free flour

5 g/1^1/$_4$ teaspoons baking powder

^{1}/$_4$ teaspoon xanthan gum

^{1}/$_4$ teaspoon salt

1 teaspoon mixed spice/apple pie spice

100 g/^{1}/$_2$ cup Victoria Sponge Cake crumbs (see page 71) or gluten-free white breadcrumbs

125 g/^{1}/$_2$ cup vegetable shortening, frozen and coarsely grated

1 medium carrot, finely grated

pouring cream, to serve

a 1.5-litre/50-oz. capacity pudding basin, greased

SERVES 6–8

Soak the fruits overnight – put the sultanas/golden raisins, dark raisins, Zante currants, mixed peel and cherries into a bowl and add the brandy. Stir and cover with clingfilm/plastic wrap. Set aside.

Cover the bottom of the pudding basin with a disc of baking parchment. Cut 2 discs of baking parchment the same size as the top of the basin.

In a large bowl, or the bowl of a free-standing mixer, whisk together the eggs and sugar until pale. Add the flour, baking powder, xanthan gum, salt, mixed spice/apple pie spice and cake or breadcrumbs, and whisk again. Add the vegetable shortening, grated carrot and soaked fruits, along with any remaining brandy, and stir until everything is well combined.

Pour the mixture into the prepared pudding basin and level the top with the back of a spoon or spatula. Lay the extra discs of baking parchment over the top of the basin, followed by a piece of foil with a pleat in the middle to allow it to expand a little. Secure the foil by tying with string.

To steam the pudding, position an upturned saucer at the bottom of a large saucepan and place the pudding basin on top – foil side facing upwards. Fill the pan with boiling water to almost halfway up the side of the basin, then cover the pan and set over a low heat for 5 hours. Check the water regularly and top up as required.

After 5 hours, remove the pan from the heat and carefully lift out of the pudding basin to cool. You can turn the pudding out and serve once it has cooled down slightly, but I would recommend baking the pudding ahead by about 4 weeks and intermittently feeding it with a little extra brandy.

To keep until required, allow to cool and, leaving the pudding in the basin, remove the foil and wrap the whole thing in clingfilm/plastic wrap. Set aside for up to month, then remove the clingfilm/plastic wrap, re-foil and steam as before for 1 hour before serving with pouring cream.

Note This is lovely served with brandy cream – whip together 250 g/1 cup of double/heavy cream with 2 tablespoons of icing/confectioners' sugar until soft peaks form, then whisk in 50 g/3^1/$_2$ tablespoons of brandy.

Devised to satisfy the cravings of a dear friend, this is not technically a malt loaf, as traditional malt extract is made from barley. Instead, this recipe uses brown teff flour and molasses to impart a similar flavour. Laden with dried fruit, it feels almost nutritious enough for a quick breakfast, or you can slice and serve with lashings of slightly salted butter and a cup of tea for an afternoon pick-me-up. The loaf can be served as soon as it's cool enough, but ideally, wrap and keep for 24–48 hours before slicing, to allow the stickiness to intensify.

From start to serve: 24 hours | Prep: 15 minutes | Bake: 1 hour | Difficulty: ●○○○○

'malt' loaf

150 g/1 cup chopped dried dates

220 ml/1 scant cup hot black tea, made with 2 tea bags

100 ml/6$^{1}/_{2}$ tablespoons black treacle/molasses

50 g/$^{1}/_{4}$ cup soft light brown sugar

115 g/$^{3}/_{4}$ cup brown teff flour

115 g/$^{3}/_{4}$ cup plain/all-purpose gluten-free flour

1 teaspoon baking powder

$^{1}/_{2}$ teaspoon xanthan gum

$^{1}/_{4}$ teaspoon salt

15 g/1 tablespoon sunflower oil

2 eggs

175 g/1 generous cup sultanas/golden raisins

butter, softened, to serve (optional)

a 900-g/2-lb. capacity loaf pan greased and lined with baking parchment

SERVES 8–10

Preheat the oven to 170°C (325°F) Gas 3.

Put the dates and tea into a saucepan and bring to a simmer over a gentle heat for 5 minutes until the dates have softened.

Remove from the heat and, using a stick blender, blitz for 30 seconds–1 minute until just about smooth.

If you don't have a stick blender, allow the dates to simmer for a further 5–10 minutes, remove from the heat and continue without blending them.

Stir in the treacle/molasses and brown sugar until well combined, then add the flours, baking powder, xanthan gum, salt, oil and eggs. Beat with a wooden spoon until smooth – the batter will be quite thick!

Stir in the sultanas/golden raisins, then transfer the mixture to the prepared loaf pan. Level and bake in the preheated oven for 1 hour, checking after 50 minutes that the top of the loaf isn't browning too much. Cover with foil if so.

Take the loaf out of the oven once it feels firm and allow to cool in the pan. Brush the top of the cake with extra treacle/molasses while still warm.

Remove the loaf from the pan when cool and, ideally, wrap in baking parchment and foil. Allow to rest for a day or two before eating. Malt loaf should be served with softened butter to spread onto slices at the table.

Note Malt loaf can be sliced and lightly toasted to serve warm, if desired, or to bring it back to life if it has become a little stale.

360 ml/1½ cups whole milk

21 g/1½ tablespoons sunflower oil

3 eggs

1 teaspoon vanilla extract

390 g/2⅔ cups plain/all-purpose gluten-free flour

21 g/5¼ teaspoons baking powder

½ teaspoon salt

½ teaspoon xanthan gum

375 g/1¾ cups plus 2 tablespoons caster/granulated sugar

105 g/7 tablespoons unsalted butter, softened

a few drops of pink gel food colouring

MARZIPAN

200 g/1 cup caster/granulated sugar

200 g/1⅔ cups icing/confectioners' sugar, plus extra for dusting

300 g/2 cups ground almonds

2 eggs

1 teaspoon almond extract

BUTTERCREAM

40 g/3 tablespoons unsalted butter, softened

100 g/¾ cup plus 1 tablespoon icing/confectioners' sugar

½ teaspoon vanilla extract

1 tablespoon whole milk

apricot jam/jelly, to spread

2 x 900-g/2-lb. loaf pans greased and lined with baking parchment

SERVES 10–12

Although this is a long recipe, the elements of a Battenberg cake are all simple enough to whip up. The trick here is mastering its construction, and planning the baking of the sponges a day ahead.

From start to serve: 24 hours | Prep: 1 hour | Bake: 20–25 minutes
Difficulty: ●●●●○

battenberg cake

Preheat the oven to 190°C (375°F) Gas 5.

In a jug/pitcher, combine the milk, oil, eggs and vanilla extract.

To a large bowl, or the bowl of a free-standing mixer, add the flour, baking powder, salt, xanthan gum, sugar and softened butter and, using a handheld electric whisk or a free-standing mixer, mix everything together until it resembles fine breadcrumbs. Continue to mix on a slow speed and pour in the wet ingredients. Increase the speed and mix for 3–5 minutes until the batter thickens. Spoon half of the mixture into one of the cake pans, and level with a spoon or spatula.

To the remaining mixture add a few drops of pink food colouring and mix until the colour is even. Spoon this into the other pan and level.

Bake the sponges in the preheated oven for 20–25 minutes until they are risen and spring back to the touch. Put the pans onto a wire rack to cool completely. Gently remove from the pans once cool and carefully wrap the sponges well in clingfilm/plastic wrap. Leave in a cool place overnight.

The next day, make the marzipan. Put the sugars, ground almonds, eggs and almond extract into a large bowl, or the bowl of a free-standing mixer. Beat until everything comes together as a dough, adding a little extra icing/confectioners' sugar and ground almonds if the mixture seems too wet.

For the buttercream, beat together the softened butter, icing/confectioners' sugar and vanilla extract until soft and smooth. Add the milk if required.

Unwrap the sponges. Level the tops and trim the edges so that they are straight on all sides. Divide each sponge into 2 equal strips. Check that all 4 sponge strips are the same size, and trim if required.

Using buttercream to create a thin, even layer of 'glue', sandwich together one cream and one pink sponge strip. Spread a layer of buttercream on top of these now adjoined strips and lay the remaining sponges on top, pink lying on white and white lying on pink to create a cuboid cake.

Lay a piece or overlapping pieces of clingfilm/plastic wrap larger than the cake onto the work surface and lightly dust with icing/confectioners' sugar. Place the ball of marzipan in the middle and gently press it into a disc

shape with your hands. With a rolling pin, roll out to a thickness of 5 mm/¼ inch in a roughly oblong shape that is just longer than the sponge.

Brush the marzipan all over with smooth apricot jam/jelly, then carefully place the joined sponges at one edge of the marzipan oblong.

Use the clingfilm/plastic wrap to help you roll the sponge in the marzipan so that it is completely covered. Smooth the sides gently with your hands to ensure a snug covering and a good adhesion.

At one corner of the sponge, bring the marzipan together and gently crimp to create a seam. Trim the excess with a sharp knife. Turn the cake over so that this join is concealed at the bottom.

Remove the clingfilm/plastic wrap completely and smooth over the cake again with your hands and a little more icing/confectioners' sugar. Trim the ends so that they are neat and display the pattern within.

At the stage the cake is finished and ready to serve, but if you prefer a more decorative effect you can crimp the edges at the top with a fork or your fingertips, or score diamonds gently into the top of the marzipan.

Battenberg will slice much more easily if allowed to sit, uncovered, for an hour or two to allow the marzipan to harden slightly.

PERFECT PASTRY

The banoffee pie tops many a 'favourite desserts' list. Definitely one for the sweet-toothed diner, a little banoffee pie goes a long way – but it can be stored in the fridge for a couple of days, so don't worry if you can't quite finish it all in one sitting! I recommend a crumb base here, as it makes the whole thing much easier to whip up. You can, if you prefer, use shortcrust pastry instead.

From start to serve: 4 hours | Prep: 30 minutes | Difficulty: ●●●○○

banoffee pie

300 g/10 oz. gluten-free digestive biscuits/graham crackers or 1 batch Shortcrust Pastry (see page 17), at room temperature

175 g/1½ sticks unsalted butter, melted

CARAMEL

200 g/1 cup caster/granulated sugar

100 g/6½ tablespoons unsalted butter, cubed

150 ml/²/3 cup double/heavy cream

TOPPINGS

3 ripe bananas

200 ml/1 scant cup double/heavy cream

2 tablespoons icing/confectioners' sugar

50 g/1½ oz. dark/bittersweet chocolate, grated

a 23-cm/9-inch loose-bottomed tart pan, greased and lined with pastry

SERVES 8–10

To begin, make the base. This is most easily done using a food processor: put the biscuits/graham crackers into it and whizz until they are in fine crumbs. Pour in the melted butter and mix until completely combined. You can make the base by hand by placing the biscuits in a plastic food bag wrapped in a tea towel and bashing with a rolling pin until you reach a crumb consistency, then transfer to a mixing bowl and stir in the melted butter with a wooden spoon.

Press the mixture evenly into the bottom and halfway up the sides of the prepared tart pan and put in the fridge while you make the top of the pie.

For the caramel, put the sugar in a large heavy-bottomed saucepan and whisk over a medium heat until completely melted. Allow to cook, continuing to whisk, until the sugar has turned caramel in colour. Remove the pan from the heat and add the cubed butter and whisk until combined. Then slowly pour in the cream and whisk again. Set aside and allow to cool for 10 minutes before pouring into the lined tart pan, then returning to the fridge to set.

After 2–3 hours, once the caramel has set, carefully remove the pie from the case and place onto a serving stand or plate.

Slice the bananas and arrange over the caramel.

Whisk together the cream and icing/confectioners' sugar until fluffy peaks form. Spread over the top of the bananas and then top with the grated chocolate.

Note Any plain gluten-free biscuit will work here but if using an unsweetened cracker-style biscuit, add a few tablespoons of caster/granulated sugar before the melted butter. If using pastry and you haven't taken the pastry from the fridge in advance, give it a 15–20 second blast in the microwave before kneading. Line and blind bake the pastry case following the instructions on page 85.

Made with maple syrup and toasted pecan nuts, this is a sticky and intensely sweet tart that makes the perfect end to a celebratory meal. It's best served at room temperature, which means it can be made in advance, leaving you more time to get on with the main event.

From start to serve: 2 hours | Prep: 30 minutes | Bake: 30–40 minutes | Difficulty: ●●●○○

pecan pie

1 batch Shortcrust Pastry (see page 17), at room temperature

350 g/2$^1/_3$ cups pecan nuts

75 g/5 tablespoons unsalted butter, cubed

100 ml/6$^1/_2$ tablespoons golden syrup/light corn syrup

50 ml/3 tablespoons maple syrup

3 eggs

225 g/1 packed cup light soft brown sugar

1 teaspoon vanilla extract

1 tablespoon plain/all-purose gluten-free flour

$^1/_2$ teaspoon salt

a 23-cm/9-inch loose-bottomed tart pan, greased and lined with baking parchment

a baking sheet lined with baking parchment

SERVES 8–12

Preheat the oven to 190°C (375°F) Gas 5.

Lay a piece or overlapping pieces of clingfilm/plastic wrap larger than your tart pan onto the work surface and lightly dust with flour. Place the pastry ball in the middle and gently press it into a disc shape with your hands. Lay a second piece of clingfilm/plastic wrap over the top of the pastry and, with a rolling pin, roll out the pastry to a thickness of 5 mm/$^1/_4$ inch in a roughly circular shape of around 30–35 cm/12–14 inches in diameter.

Lift off the top layer of clingfilm/plastic wrap and, using the rolling pin to help lift the pastry, lay the pastry over the pan, so that the remaining clingfilm/plastic wrap is facing upwards. Gently lift and press the pastry into the pan, easing it into the corners. Remove the clingfilm/plastic wrap and trim the excess away from the pan. If there are any cracks in the pastry, use the trimmings to patch them back together – and don't panic!

Chill the pastry case in the fridge while you make the filling.

Spread the pecan nuts in one layer onto the lined baking sheet and bake in the preheated oven for 5–8 minutes until lightly toasted. Keep the oven on.

Cool slightly and then chop 200 g/scant 2 cups of the now toasted nuts, leaving the remainder in whole pieces.

In a saucepan gently melt together the butter and both syrups until completely combined. Then remove from the heat and set aside.

In a large bowl, or the bowl of a free-standing mixer, whisk together the eggs and sugar until pale. Add the butter and syrup mixture along with the vanilla extract, flour and salt, and whisk again. Stir in the chopped nuts and pour into the chilled pastry case.

Arrange the remaining nuts over the top of the tart in concentric circles and then bake in the oven for 30–40 minutes until the filling has set.

Remove from the oven and allow to cool completely in the pan before carefully removing. The tart slices can be served cool or warmed in the oven for a few minutes before serving.

Note If you haven't taken the pastry from the fridge in advance, give it a 15–20 second blast in the microwave before kneading.

Once you've mastered choux pastry, buns or 'cream puffs' become easy and you can attempt this French celebration bake. A pyramid of profiteroles filled with a boozy cream and secured with caramel, it looks lovely, tastes delicious and is quicker to make than a traditional cake. Assemble no more than a couple of hours before serving, as the caramel and spun sugar will disintegrate.

From start to serve: 2 hours | Prep: 45 minutes | Bake: 20 minutes | Difficulty: ●●●●●

croquembouche

80 g/5^{1}/$_{2}$ tablespoons unsalted butter

40 ml/3 tablespoons whole milk

125 g/^{3}/$_{4}$ cup plus 2 tablespoons plain/all-purpose gluten-free flour

a pinch of salt

4 eggs, beaten

300 ml/1^{1}/$_{4}$ cups double/heavy cream

3 tablespoons icing/confectioners' sugar

2 teaspoons cornflour/cornstarch

2 tablespoons rum

250 g/1^{1}/$_{4}$ cups caster/granulated sugar

a piping/pastry bag fitted with a wide nozzle/tip

2 baking sheets lined with baking parchment or silicone baking sheets

a piping/pastry bag fitted with a small nozzle/tip

SERVES 8–10

Preheat the oven to 220°C (425°F) Gas 7.

In a pan set over a low heat, melt together the butter, 110 ml/scant ^{1}/$_{2}$ cup of water and the milk. Bring just to the boil. Remove the pan from the heat and beat in the flour and salt, tipping it all in in one go. Return to the heat briefly, beating the mixture until it comes together in a thick dough. Tip the mixture into a large bowl and allow to rest for 5 minutes to cool slightly.

Using an electric handwhisk or in a free-standing mixer, add the eggs, a small amount at a time, beating well after each addition. Continue to add the eggs, and once you have beaten them all in with the mixer, switch to a wooden spoon and beat vigorously for another 1–2 minutes until you have a smooth paste that drops slowly from a spoon. Transfer the mixture into the piping/pastry bag fitted with the wide nozzle/tip.

Pipe the choux paste in large walnut-sized blobs onto the prepared baking sheets and bake in the preheated oven for 15 minutes until risen and golden. The tops should feel crisp when lightly tapped. Turn them over and return to the oven for 3–5 minutes to ensure they are crisped all over. Cool completely on a wire rack before filling.

Whisk together the cream, icing/confectioners' sugar and cornflour/cornstarch until almost stiff. Add the rum and whisk again, then transfer to the piping/pastry bag fitted with the small nozzle/tip. Poke a hole in the bottom of each choux bun, push in the nozzle/tip and fill with the cream.

Put the caster/granulated sugar into a heavy-bottomed saucepan with 1 tablespoon of water. Stir and then cook over a low heat without any further stirring until the sugar is dissolved. Increase the heat slightly and cook the sugar syrup for about 5 minutes until it is a rich caramel colour. Remove from the heat. Very carefully dip one side of each bun into the molten caramel and arrange in a pyramid tower on a serving plate.

Spoon over some of the remaining caramel to glaze the outside of the buns and help to solidify the structure. Return the caramel to the heat to liquify, then use a fork to flick strands of sugar over the handle of a wooden spoon to create strands of spun sugar. Gather up and drape over the pyramid.

A lovely dessert and an American classic, this pumpkin pie is excellent served with a simple drizzle of cream and can be eaten hot or cold. I have been a little roguish here and used butternut squash instead of pumpkin, because it's far easier to get hold of year-round in the UK. There's no compromise, as the flavour is perfectly akin to the canned pumpkin that is normal for this recipe in the US.

From start to serve: 3 hours | Prep: 30 minutes | Bake: 40-50 minutes | Difficulty: ●●●○○

pumpkin pie

1 batch Shortcrust Pastry (see page 17), at room temperature (If you haven't taken the pastry from the fridge in advance, give it a 15–20 second blast in the microwave before kneading.)

1 medium butternut squash

2 eggs

150 g/^{3}/$_4$ cup caster/granulated sugar

30 g/2 tablespoons unsalted butter, melted

150 ml/^{2}/$_3$ cup evaporated milk

2 teaspoons mixed spice/apple pie spice

^{1}/$_2$ teaspoon salt

a 23-cm/9-inch loose-bottomed tart pan, greased

SERVES 8–12

Preheat the oven to 190°C (375°F) Gas 5.

Lay a piece or overlapping pieces of clingfilm/platic wrap larger than your tart pan onto the work surface and lightly dust with plain/all-purpose gluten-free flour. Put the pastry ball in the middle and gently press into a disc shape with your hands. Lay a second piece of clingfilm/plastic wrap over the top and, with a rolling pin, roll out the pastry to a thickness of 5 mm/^{1}/$_4$ inch in a roughly circular shape of around 30–35 cm/12–14 inches in diameter.

Lift off the top layer of clingfilm/plastic wrap and, using the rolling pin to help lift it, lay the pastry over the pan, so that the remaining clingfilm/plastic wrap is facing upwards.

Gently lift and press the pastry into the pan, easing it into the corners. Then remove the clingfilm/plastic wrap. Trim away the excess and if there are any cracks in the pastry, use the trimmings to patch them back together – and don't panic! Put the pastry case in the fridge while you make the filling.

Peel, seed and chop the butternut squash into largish chunks. Put into a pan, cover with water and bring to the boil. Cook for 15–20 minutes, until tender, then drain into a colander. Set the colander aside and allow the squash to cool in it, this will allow the excess water to drain away as it cools.

Push the cooled squash through a sturdy, fine-mesh sieve/strainer into a bowl. Discard the fibrous squash that remains in the sieve/strainer.

To another large bowl, or the bowl of a free-standing mixer, add the eggs and sugar. Use a handhled electric whisk or the whisk attachment to slowly mix together until pale. Add the melted butter, spices, salt and evaporated milk, followed by the squash purée.

Pour the filling into the prepared tart case, place onto a baking sheet and bake in the preheated oven for 40–50 minutes until the filling is set.

Remove from the oven and allow to cool completely in the pan before carefully removing and serving in generous slices.

Although this recipe takes its name from the Florida Keys' limes that it is traditionally made with, any fresh, juicy limes will do just fine. Zingy and light, it makes a wonderful dinner-party dessert, as it can be made ahead and stored in the fridge until serving.

From start to serve: 5 hours | Prep: 30 minutes | Bake: 30 minutes | Difficulty: ●●○○○

key lime pie

2 tablespoons melted butter, for greasing

175 g/1½ sticks unsalted butter, melted

300 g/10 oz. gluten-free digestive biscuits/graham crackers (see Note)

3 egg yolks

zest and freshly squeezed juice of 4 large limes

a 397-g/14-oz. can of sweetened condensed milk

350 ml/1½ cups double/heavy cream

2 tablespoons icing/confectioners' sugar

a 23-cm/9-inch springform tart pan lightly greased with melted butter

SERVES 8

Preheat the oven to 180°C (350°F) Gas 4.

To begin, make the base. This is most easily done using a food processor: put the biscuits/graham crackers into it and whizz until they are in fine crumbs. Pour in the melted butter and mix until completely combined. You can make the base by hand by placing the biscuits/crackers in a plastic food bag wrapped in a kitchen cloth and bashing with a rolling pin until you reach a crumb consistency, then transfer to a mixing bowl and stir in the melted butter with a wooden spoon. Press the mixture evenly into the bottom and halfway up the sides of the prepared tart pan. Bake in the preheated oven for 10 minutes, then remove and set aside to cool. Keep the oven on – the whole pie will be going back in!

To a large bowl, or the bowl of a free-standing mixer, add the egg yolks and lime zest, reserving a little to garnish if desired. Whisk together for a minute and then add the lime juice and condensed milk. Whisk for 3–4 minutes until smooth.

Pour the topping onto the now slightly cooled base, then put the whole thing back into the oven and bake for 15–20 minutes until the mixture feels set.

Put the pan onto a wire rack and allow to cool for at least an hour. Refrigerate for a further 3 hours, minimum, but preferably overnight.

When ready to serve, whip the double/heavy cream with the icing/confectioners' sugar until standing in soft peaks. Then, gently remove the pie from the pan and transfer to a serving plate. Dress the top with clouds of whipped cream, or pipe for a more refined appearance. You can add a little freshly grated lime zest for extra pizzazz, if you like.

Variation For a lighter version, serve with pouring cream or crème fraîche instead of topping with whipped cream.

Note If you can't find digestives, any plain gluten-free biscuit/cracker will work here. If you are using an unsweetened cracker style biscuit, add a few tablespoons of caster/granulated sugar before the melted butter.

These individual tarts are deep-filled with a set egg-custard filling and finished with a sprinkling of nutmeg. The filling should be rich and luxuriously smooth, and makes for the perfect mid-afternoon treat.

From start to serve: 3 hours | Prep: 20 minutes | Bake: 40–45 minutes | Difficulty: ●●○○○

egg custard tarts

1 quantity Shortcrust Pastry (see page 17), at room temperature

1 egg

2 egg yolks

50 g/$\frac{1}{4}$ cup caster/granulated sugar

300 ml/1$\frac{1}{4}$ cups double/heavy cream

whole nutmeg, for grating

a 10-cm/4-inch round cookie cutter

a 12-hole deep muffin pan greased with butter

MAKES 10–12

Preheat the oven to 190°C (375°F) Gas 5.

Lay a piece or overlapping pieces of clingfilm/plastic wrap larger than your tart pan onto the work surface and lightly dust with plain/all-purpose gluten-free flour. Put the pastry ball in the middle and gently press into a disc shape with your hands. Lay a second piece of clingfilm/plastic wrap over the top and, with a rolling pin, roll out the pastry quite thinly.

Remove the top layer of clingfilm/plastic wrap. Stamp out discs using the cookie cutter, then gently lift and press each disc into a hole of the prepared pan, easing it into the corners. Re-roll the trimmings until all the holes are lined. If you want to, trim the excess away from the top of the pan, but it can look nice to simply ruffle the pastry edges slightly.

If there are any cracks in the pastry, use the trimmings to patch them back together – as ever, don't panic! Bake the pastry cups in the preheated oven for 20 minutes, until beginning to turn golden.

Meanwhile, make the custard filling. Whisk together the egg, egg yolks and sugar in a jug/pitcher. Heat the cream until simmering in a saucepan over a medium heat, then pour over the eggs and sugar, whisking to combine. Set aside to cool.

Remove the pastry cups from the oven and set aside. Turn the oven down to 170°C (325°F) Gas 3.

Strain the egg-custard filling into a fresh jug/pitcher, then pour into the pastry cups. Once they are all filled, grate fresh nutmeg over the tops of all the tarts, so they are lightly dusted, then return to the oven to bake for a further 20–25 mintues.

Check the tarts are done by jiggling the pan slightly: the filling should be set. Allow to cool completely in the tin, on a wire rack, before carefully removing. Store, covered, in the fridge for up to 3 days.

Note If you haven't taken the pastry from the fridge in advance, give it a 15–20 second blast in the microwave before kneading. You can bake a large custard tart, if you prefer. Line a 23-cm/9-inch tart pan with the pastry, blind bake for 20 minutes (see page 14) and bake with the filling for 45–50 minutes.

A beautiful almond tart with a layer of sweet raspberry jam/jelly. Most recipes recommend blind baking the tart case first, but I find it has a tendency to crack. So, instead, I opt for a longer, slower bake of the whole tart, which ensures you avoid the dreaded 'soggy bottom' and the case remains intact for perfect slicing.

From start to serve: 2 hours | Prep: 30 minutes | Bake: 35–45 minutes | Difficulty: ●●●○○

bakewell tart

1 batch Shortcrust Pastry (see page 17), at room temperature

150 g/^{2}/$_3$ cup raspberry jam/jelly

2 tablespoons flaked/slivered almonds

pouring cream, to serve (optional)

FRANGIPANE

200 g/1 stick plus 5 tablespoons tablespoons unsalted butter

200 g/1 cup caster/granulated sugar

2 eggs

200 g/1^1/$_3$ cups ground almonds

75 g/^{1}/$_2$ cup plain/all-purpose gluten-free flour

5 g/1^1/$_4$ teaspoons baking powder

2 teaspoons almond extract (optional)

a 23-cm/9-inch loose-bottomed tart pan greased with softened butter

SERVES 8

Preheat the oven to 180°C (350°F) Gas 4.

Lay a piece or overlapping pieces of clingfilm/plastic wrap larger than your tart pan onto the work surface and lightly dust with plain/all-purpose gluten-free flour. Put the pastry ball in the middle and gently press into a disc shape with your hands. Lay a second piece of clingfilm/plastic wrap over the top and, with a rolling pin, roll out the pastry to a thickness of 5 mm/^{1}/$_4$ inch in a roughly circular shape of around 30–35 cm/12–14 inches in diameter. Lift off the top layer of clingfilm/plastic wrap and, using the rolling pin to help lift it, lay the pastry over the pan, so that the remaining clingfilm/plastic wrap is facing upwards.

Gently lift and press the pastry into the pan, easing it into the corners. Then remove the clingfilm/plastic wrap. Trim away the excess and if there are any cracks in the pastry, use the trimmings to patch them back together – and don't panic! Put the pastry case in the fridge while you make the filling.

For the frangipane, in a large bowl and using a wooden spoon, or in a free-standing mixer, cream the butter and sugar until pale and fluffy. Creaming the butter and sugar well for the frangipane filling will ensure your tart isn't heavy or cloying. Just a splash of almond extract enhances the flavour, but if you don't have it to hand, it's not a deal-breaker to leave it out. Add the eggs, ground almonds, flour, baking powder and almond extract and mix well until combined.

Take the pastry case from the fridge and cover the base with a generous layer of raspberry jam/jelly using the back of a spoon. Be sure not to cut through the base when spreading it out. Top with the frangipane filling and level with a spatula, sealing the edges of the tart case with the mixture so no jam/jelly is visible. Sprinkle the flaked/slivered almonds on top and bake, on a baking tray, in the preheated oven for 35–40 minutes until the filling is golden and set.

Allow to cool completely in the pan before removing carefully and slicing. Serve with pouring cream if desired.

Note If you haven't taken the pastry from the fridge in advance, give it a 15–20 second blast in the microwave before kneading.

Akin to an upside-down apple pie, this classic French caramelized apple tart looks extremely impressive, but is actually fairly straightforward to make. Deliver this tart to the table whole, as once sliced it won't hold its shape. It will taste absolutely divine served with caramel ice cream or crème fraîche.

From start to serve: 1 hour | Prep: 20 minutes | Bake: 30 minutes | Difficulty: ●●●○○

tarte tatin

200 g/1 cup caster/
granulated sugar

50 g/3 tablespoons unsalted
butter, cubed

2 Cox's apples, peeled,
cored and thinly sliced

3 Granny Smith apples,
peeled, cored and thinly
sliced

1/2 batch Shortcrust Pastry
(see page 17), at room
temperature (If you haven't
taken the pastry from the
fridge in advance, give it
a 15–20 second blast in the
microwave before kneading)

*a 20-cm/8-inch ovenproof
frying pan/skillet*

SERVES 6

Preheat the oven to 190°C (375°F) Gas 5.

Put the sugar into the ovenproof frying pan/skillet and add 50 ml/1/4 cup of water. Stir to combine. Set the pan over a medium heat, and without further stirring, bring the sugar to a simmer and allow to cook for 5–10 minutes until golden and caramelized. Remove the pan from the heat and add the cubed butter. Whisk until fully combined.

Carefully, being sure not to touch the caramel at all, arrange the apple slices over sauce in the pan in a circular pattern, overlapping and distributing the two apple types evenly.

Return the pan to the heat and allow to cook for a further 5 minutes, to colour the underside of the apples. Turn off the heat, and leave the pan undisturbed.

Lightly knead the room-temperature pastry on a clean, cool work surface. Lay a piece of clingfilm/plastic wrap larger than your pan onto the work surface. Place the pastry ball in the middle and gently press it into a disc shape with your hands. Lay a second piece of clingfilm/plastic wrap over the top and roll out the pastry to a thickness of 5 mm/1/4 inch in a roughly circular shape just larger than the pan.

Remove the top layer of clingfilm/plastic wrap and gently lift and press the pastry into the pan, so the remaining clingfilm is now on top of the pastry. Remove this and carefully tuck the excess down into the sides of the apples to encase them from the underside.

Put the pan into the preheated oven and bake for 30 minutes until the pastry is golden. Remove and set aside to rest for 15–20 minutes.

Take a serving plate larger than the pan and place on top of the pan. Using oven gloves to protect your hands, invert the pan onto the plate. Tap the bottom a few times sharply, then lift away the pan – the tart should come away wholly with some caramel sauce still oozing from the apples. Deliver to the table whole, and serve warm.

Note I can't stress enough that you must be careful and keep your wits about you during the cooking process for this tart, as the molten caramel is dangerously hot and could impart a nasty burn.

Made with golden syrup/light corn syrup rather than black treacle/molasses, this is a gloriously sticky tart. I include this in my 'waste not, want not' category of baking, as it calls for cake crumbs in the filling and there is often something knocking about the kitchen that can be used to make these. I recommend crumbs from the Victoria Sponge Cake (see page 71), as they are gorgeously soft and make the filling extra moist, simply break up your spare cake or cake trimmings, pop into a food processor and whizz to crumb consistency.

From start to serve: 2 hours | Prep: 30 minutes | Bake: 40–45 minutes | Difficulty: ●●●○○

treacle tart

1 batch Shortcrust Pastry (see page 17), at room temperature (if you haven't taken the pastry from the fridge in advance, give it a 15–20 second blast in the microwave before kneading)

350 ml golden syrup/1 cup light corn syrup mixed with $^1/_3$ cup molasses

150 ml/$^2/_3$ cup double/heavy cream

1 egg

2 teaspoons lemon juice

120 g/2 cups gluten-free cake crumbs

55 g/$^1/_3$ cup ground almonds

clotted cream, to serve

a 23-cm/9-inch loosed-bottomed tart pan, greased

SERVES 8–12

Preheat the oven to 180°C (350°F) Gas 4.

Lay a piece or overlapping pieces of clingfilm/plastic wrap larger than your tart pan onto the work surface and lightly dust with plain/all-purpose gluten-free flour. Put the pastry ball in the middle and gently press into a disc shape with your hands. Lay a second piece of clingfilm/plastic wrap over the top and, with a rolling pin, roll out the pastry to a thickness of 5 mm/$^1/_4$ inch in a roughly circular shape of around 30–35 cm/ 12–14 inches in diameter.

Lift off the top layer of clingfilm/plastic wrap and, using the rolling pin to help lift it, lay the pastry over the pan, so that the remaining clingfilm/ plastic wrap is facing upwards.

Gently lift and press the pastry into the pan, easing it into the corners. Then remove the clingfilm/plastic wrap. Trim away the excess and if there are any cracks in the pastry, use the trimmings to patch them back together – and don't panic! Put the pastry case in the fridge while you make the filling.

For the filling, in a large bowl or in a free-standing mixer, whisk the syrup, cream, egg and lemon juice together until combined. Add the crumbs and ground almonds and whisk again until no lumps remain.

Pour the filling into the pastry case and bake, on a baking tray, in the preheated oven for 40–45 minutes until the filling is golden brown and set.

Check the tart after 30 minutes; if the top is starting to colour too much and the filling is not yet nearly set, turn the oven down to 150°C (300°F) Gas 2 and allow to bake for a little longer than the specified time.

Cool completely in the pan before removing carefully and slicing. If you have time, place the tart still in its pan into the fridge for an hour or so once it has cooled to make portioning the tart much easier. Serve with clotted cream for delicious indulgence.

If you bring this tart to the table you are almost guaranteed a round of applause. Not only does it look amazing, the combination of flavours here is fantastic – zesty lemon and super-sweet meringue are a match made in heaven. It is best made and served on the same day, as the meringue can start to seep.

From start to serve: 4 hours | Prep: 30 minutes | Bake: 30 minutes | Difficulty: ●●●○○

lemon meringue tart

1 batch Shortcrust Pastry (see page 17), at room temperature (if you haven't taken the pastry from the fridge in advance, give it a 15–20 second blast in the microwave before kneading)

LEMON FILLING

150 g/^{3}/$_4$ cup caster/granulated sugar

50 g/^{1}/$_2$ cup cornflour/cornstarch

zest and freshly squeezed juice of 4 lemons

4 egg yolks

50 g/3^1/$_2$ tablespoons unsalted butter, cubed

MERINGUE TOPPING

3 egg whites

175 g/1 cup caster/superfine sugar

a 23-cm/9-inch loosed-bottomed tart pan, greased

SERVES 8–12

Preheat the oven to 190°C (375°F) Gas 5.

Lay a piece or overlapping pieces of clingfilm/platic wrap larger than your tart pan onto the work surface and lightly dust with plain/all-purpose gluten-free flour. Put the pastry ball in the middle and gently press into a disc shape with your hands. Lay a second piece of clingfilm/plastic wrap over the top and, with a rolling pin, roll out the pastry to a thickness of 5 mm/^{1}/$_4$ inch in a roughly circular shape of around 30–35 cm/12–14 inches in diameter.

Lift off the top layer of clingfilm/plastic wrap and, using the rolling pin to help lift it, lay the pastry over the pan, so that the remaining clingfilm/plastic wrap is facing upwards. Gently lift and press the pastry into the pan, easing it into the corners. Then remove the clingfilm/plastic wrap. Trim away the excess and if there are any cracks in the pastry, use the trimmings to patch them back together.

Lay a piece of baking parchment over the pastry case and cover with baking beans. Place onto a baking sheet and blind bake in the preheated oven for 15 minutes. Remove the beans and baking parchment, then return to the oven to bake for another 5–10 minutes until golden. Remove from the oven and set aside to cool. Reduce the oven to 170°C (325°F) Gas 3.

In a bowl mix together the sugar and cornflour/cornstarch and add 3 tablespoons of the lemon juice. Mix to form a paste. Put the remaining lemon juice into a saucepan with 400 ml/1^3/$_4$ cups of water and the lemon zest and bring to the boil. Pour in the cornflour/cornstarch paste, whisking until completely combined, then remove the pan from the heat. Whisk in the egg yolks and butter until melted, then return to a low heat, stirring until thickened. Pour into the baked pastry case and set aside.

In a spotlessly clean bowl, whisk the egg whites until they are stiff. Add the sugar, a heaped tablespoon at a time, whisking until fully incorporated. Once all the sugar has been added, the meringue should be very thick and shiny. Use a spatula to spoon and spread the meringue over the lemon curd filling, making sure that it covers the whole top and meets the pastry to form a seal. Use the spoon to lift into peaks and swirls on top.

Bake for 20–25 minutes until the meringue is crisp and golden. Allow to cool in the pan before removing to serve.

For many of our customers at 2 Oxford Place, special occasions are when they miss their favourite bakes the most. They can go eleven months unfazed by fruit salads, but come December, the denial of a mince pie is really a step too far. You might not be able to buy gluten-free everywhere you go, but armed with these beauties and a Tupperware, you need never go without.

From start to serve: 1 hour | Prep: 30 minutes | Bake 15–20 minutes | Difficulty: ●●○○○

mince pies

1 batch Shortcrust Pastry (see page 17), at room temperature

350 g/12 oz. gluten-free mincemeat

2 tablespoons brandy (optional)

1 beaten egg, to glaze

icing/confectioners' sugar, to dust

a 10-cm/4-inch round cookie cutter

a star or round 7.5-cm/3-inch cookie cutter

a 12-hole muffin pan, greased

MAKES 12

Preheat the oven to 190°C (375°F) Gas 5.

Lightly knead the room-temperature pastry on a clean, cool work surface and then divide into two pieces, one that is roughly double the size of the other. Lay a large piece of clingfilm/plastic wrap onto the work surface and lightly dust with plain/all-purpose gluten-free flour. Place the larger pastry ball in the middle and gently press it into a disc shape with your hands.

Lay a second piece of clingfilm/plastic wrap over the top and, with a rolling pin, roll out the pastry quite thinly.

Remove the top layer of clingfilm/plastic wrap. Stamp out discs using the cookie cutter, gently lifting and press each disc into a hole of the prepared pan, easing it into the corners. Re-roll the trimmings until all the pastry is used up and all of the pan is lined. If there are any cracks in the pastry, use the trimmings to patch them back together – as ever, don't panic!

In a bowl mix together the mincemeat and brandy (if using), then spoon a heaped teaspoon of the mixture into each pastry case.

Repeat the rolling-out process for the remaining piece of pastry and then use a star or smaller cutter to cut out festive lids for the pies and place on top. Brush the tops with the beaten egg and bake in the preheated oven for 15–20 minutes until golden brown.

Put the pan onto a wire rack and allow the mince pies to cool before serving. If you try to take them from the pan too soon the risk of the mince pies breaking is much higher. Once they are cooled, be delicate when removing these from the pan, and loosen the edges with a table or small palette knife if required.

Dust with icing/confectioners' sugar before serving. Store in an airtight container for up to 3 days.

Note If you haven't taken the pastry from the fridge in advance, give it a 15–20 second blast in the microwave before kneading.

With a little practice, choux paste is very achievable and actually quite quick to make. Ensure that you have everything weighed out in advance, your equipment all to hand and the oven hot. You'll also need nerves of steel as it progresses through worrying stages of peculiarity, but stick with it.

From start to serve: 3 hours | Prep: 20 minutes | Bake: 15–20 minutes | Difficulty: ●●●●○

chocolate éclairs

80 g/5^1/$_2$ tablespoons unsalted butter

40 g/3 tablespoons whole milk

125 g/^{3}/$_4$ cup plus 2 tablespoons plain/ all-purpose gluten-free flour

a pinch of salt

4 eggs, beaten

125 g/4 oz. dark/bittersweet chocolate

20 g/1 tablespoon plus 1 teaspoon unsalted butter

50 ml/3 tablespoons double/ heavy cream

coloured writing icing (optional)

CHOCOLATE GLAZE

300 ml/1^1/$_3$ cups double/ heavy cream

2 tablespoons icing/ confectioners' sugar

1 teaspoon cornflour/ cornstarch

2 baking sheets lined with baking parchment or silicone baking sheets

a piping/pastry bag fitted with a wide nozzle/tip

a piping/pastry bag fitted with a medium nozzle/tip

MAKES 8–10

Preheat the oven to 220°C (425°F) Gas 7.

In a pan set over a low heat, melt together the butter, 110 ml/scant ^{1}/$_2$ cup of water and milk. Bring just to the boil. Remove the pan from the heat and beat in the flour and salt, tipping it all in in one go. Return to the heat briefly, beating the mixture until it comes together in a thick dough. Tip the mixture into a large bowl and allow to rest for 5 minutes, to cool slightly.

Using an electric handwhisk or in a free-standing mixer, add the eggs, a small amount at a time, beating well after each addition. Your mixture will look like scrambled eggs to begin with, and for much of this process. Keep adding and beating and it will come together! Continue to add the eggs, and once you have beaten them all in with the mixer, switch to a wooden spoon and beat vigorously for another 1–2 minutes until you have a smooth paste that drops slowly from a spoon. Transfer the mixture into the piping/ pastry bag fitted with the wide nozzle/tip.

Pipe the choux paste onto the prepared baking sheets in 10–14-cm/ 4–6-inch lines, spacing well apart.

Bake in the preheated oven for 15–20 minutes until risen and golden. The tops should feel crisp when lightly tapped.

Transfer to a wire rack to cool completely before filling.

Melt together the dark/bittersweet chocolate and butter in a bowl set over a pan of simmering water or using the microwave. Whisk in the double/ heavy cream and set aside to cool slightly.

Whisk together the cream, icing/confectioners' sugar and cornflour/ cornstarch until stiff. Transfer to the piping/pastry bag fitted with the medium nozzle/tip.

Slice along the side of each éclair to form a pocket and generously pipe in the cream. Spread the chocolate topping over the top of the éclairs, and allow to set before serving. Drizzle with coloured writing icing, if desired.

Discovering the combination of chocolate with cardamom was a euphoric moment for me. I am officially a chocaholic, but I can appreciate that this combination might not be for everyone, so this recipe will work as a straight-up chocolate tart too, just skip the step for infusing the cream.

From start to serve: 4 hours | Prep: 30 minutes | Bake: 25 minutes | Set: 4 hours | Difficulty: ●●●○○

chocolate and cardamom tart

8–10 cardamom pods

400 g/1¾ cups double/heavy cream

100 g/½ cup caster/granulated sugar

1 batch plain or chocolate-flavoured Shortcrust Pastry (see page 16), at room temperature (If you haven't taken the pastry from the fridge in advance, give it a 15–20 second blast in the microwave before kneading.)

375 g/12½ oz. dark/bittersweet chocolate, chopped (minimum 60% cocoa solids)

50 g/3½ tablespoons unsalted butter, in cubes

a 23-cm/9-inch loose-bottomed tart pan, greased

SERVES 8–12

Begin by infusing the cream with cardamom, if using. Crush the cardamom pods in a pestle and mortar, or using a heavy rolling pin, then put into a saucepan with the cream and sugar. Bring to a simmer over a low heat for a minute or two, then transfer to a jug/pitcher and cover with clingfilm/plastic wrap. Leave to infuse for at least 30 minutes.

Preheat the oven to 190°C (375°F) Gas 5.

Lightly knead the room-temperature pastry on a clean, cool work surface.

Lay a piece or overlapping pieces of clingfilm/plastic wrap larger than your tart pan onto the work surface and lightly dust with plain/all-purpose gluten-free flour. Put the pastry ball in the middle and gently press into a disc shape with your hands. Lay a second piece of clingfilm/plastic wrap over the top and, with a rolling pin, roll out the pastry to a thickness of 5 mm/¼ inch in a roughly circular shape of around 30–35 cm/12–14 inches in diameter.

Lift off the top layer of clingfilm/plastic wrap and, using the rolling pin to help lift it, lay the pastry over the pan, so that the remaining clingfilm/plastic wrap is facing upwards.

Gently lift and press the pastry into the pan, easing it into the corners. Then remove the clingfilm/plastic wrap. Trim away the excess and if there are any cracks in the pastry, use the trimmings to patch them back together.

Lay a piece of baking parchment over the pastry case and cover with baking beans. Place onto a baking sheet and blind bake in the preheated oven for 15 minutes. Remove the beans and baking parchment, then return to the oven to bake for another 5–10 minutes until golden. Remove from the oven and set aside to cool. Reduce the heat to 170°C (325°F) Gas 3.

If not using infused cream, put the sugar and cream into a pan and bring to a simmer. If using the infused cardamom cream, return to a pan to re-heat.

Put the chopped chocolate and butter into a bowl and pour over the simmering cream, straining through a fine-mesh sieve/strainer if you have infused with cardamom. Whisk together for a few minutes until smooth and silky then pour into the cooled tart case. Cool slightly, then chill the tart for 3–4 hours in the fridge before serving.

DELICIOUS DESSERTS

I love being able to offer up dedicated, gluten- and dairy-free, 'proper' desserts! This is a dairy-free version of a French classic, and I really love the slightly tropical feel from the coconut cream. If you aren't avoiding dairy, you can use regular double/heavy cream instead; the recipe will work equally well.

From start to serve: 3 hours | Prep: 15 minutes | Bake: 30–35 minutes | Difficulty: ●●○○○

coconut crème brûlée

25 g/2 tablespoons caster/
granulated sugar, plus extra
to top

3 egg yolks

300 ml/1¼ cups coconut
cream

1 vanilla pod/bean

a chef's blowtorch (optional)

MAKES 2–3

Preheat the oven to 170°C (325°F) Gas 3.

Place 2 large, or 3 small, ramekins into a deep baking dish and set aside.

In a large jug/pitcher, whisk together the caster/granulated sugar and egg yolks. Remove the seeds from the vanilla pod/bean, add to the mixture and whisk again. (This is done by splitting open the pod/bean lengthways and carefully running the blade of a knife along the inside of each half.)

Put the coconut cream in a pan set over a low heat until simmering.

Pour the cream into the jug/pitcher with the eggs, whisking all the time, until well combined. Pour the mixture into the ramekins until nearly full.

Fill a baking dish around the filled ramekins with tepid water, so that it reaches halfway up the sides of the ramekins, then put the whole thing into the preheated oven to bake for 30–35 minutes.

Check that the brûlées are set by giving the dish a gentle shake. There should be just a slight wobble to the custards. Remove from the oven and allow to cool before putting into the fridge for a couple of hours to chill and set completely.

When you are ready to serve, sprinkle the tops of the brûlées with caster/granulated sugar. Ideally, use a chef's blowtorch to caramelize the sugar, swirling the ramekins around as you melt the sugar so that it creates an even layer of crunchy caramel. If you don't have a blowtorch, preheat the grill/broiler to hot and place the brûlées underneath. If the custards get too hot, you can pop them back into the fridge to re-chill before serving.

Note Coconut cream can be found in most larger supermarkets, but if you can't find it, buy a couple of cans of regular coconut milk and once you have them at home, allow them to settle in a cool place for a couple of hours. The coconut cream and coconut water will separate in the can. Open, and spoon off the cream, discarding the water beneath.

Of all the desserts, a crumble warrants little by way of introduction. Once you've cracked this recipe – and it really is gloriously simple – why not mix it up with different fruits and spices – pear and ginger, apple and blackberry, rhubarb and vanilla. You can be a bit cheffy about things, too! Mix up the crumble topping separately beforehand and bake on a lined baking sheet. Once cooled, blitz in a food processor. When ready to serve, take any warm, stewed fruit, pop into a bowl and generously sprinkle over the crumble topping. Pop the dish under the grill/broiler for a few minutes and you'll have an almost instant crumble.

From start to serve: 1 hour | Prep: 15 minutes | Bake: 40–45 minutes | Difficulty: ●○○○○

apple crumble

8 medium eating apples

40 g/3 tablespoons caster/granulated sugar

1 tablespoon plain/all-purpose gluten-free flour

1 teaspoon ground cinnamon

pouring cream or dairy-free ice cream, to serve

CRUMBLE TOPPING

70 g/5 tablespoons unsalted butter or dairy-free spread, softened

140 g/1 scant cup plain/all-purpose gluten-free flour

a pinch of salt

70 g/^{1}/$_{3}$ cup caster/granulated sugar

1 teaspoon ground cinnamon

a 20-cm/8-inch baking dish

SERVES 4–6

Preheat the oven to 190°C (375°F) Gas 5.

Peel and core the apples, then chop into 2-cm/^{3}/$_{4}$-inch chunks.

Toss the apples with a tablespoon of water, the caster/granulated sugar, flour and cinnamon, then spread evenly over the base of the baking dish. Press down lightly with your hands.

To make the crumble topping, rub together the butter and flour and a pinch of table salt until the mixture resembles rough breadcrumbs.

Stir in the sugar and cinnamon, then spread the mixture over the apples in the dish. Lightly press down the mixture so it is compact. (You can make the topping using a food processor, if you have one. Put all of the ingredients in at the same time and pulse until you have a consistency similar to breadcrumbs.)

Put the dish onto a baking sheet and bake in the preheated oven for 40–45 minutes until the crumble is golden and just brown on top.

Remove from the oven and allow to cool for a few minutes before serving with cream or dairy-free ice cream.

Note To make this crumble dairy-free, simply substitute the butter in the crumble topping for your preferred dairy-free spread and serve with dairy-free ice cream.

I know that a Pavlova is naturally gluten-free. I know that we have all seen how to make them time and time again. But it's my favourite! And a good one is, for me, an absolutely unbeatable dessert. This is my Pav recipe and hopefully you'll give it a whirl. I like to cut through the sweetness of the meringue and the richness of the cream with the addition of tart set yogurt and add passionfruit seeds for extra tang and texture.

From start to serve: 4 hours | Prep: 20 minutes | Bake: 3 hours | Difficulty: ●●○○○

perfect pavlova

4 egg whites

225 g/1 cup plus
2 tablespoons caster/
granulated sugar

1 teaspoon white wine
vinegar

1 teaspoon cornflour/
cornstarch

200 ml/^{3}/$_4$ cup double/heavy
cream

2 tablespoons icing/
confectioners' sugar, plus
extra to dust

100 ml/6^1/$_2$ tablespoons
natural set yogurt (I like
Greek yogurt)

200 g/1^1/$_3$ cups fresh
raspberries

100 g/^{2}/$_3$ cup fresh
strawberries, hulled and
quartered

2 passion fruits

fresh mint leaves

*a baking sheet lined with
baking parchment*

SERVES 8–10

Preheat the oven to 150°C (300°F) Gas 2.

In a spotlessly clean bowl, whisk the egg whites until they are stiff. Add the caster/granulated sugar, 1 heaped tablespoon at a time, whisking until fully incorporated. Once all the sugar has been added, the meringue should be very thick and shiny – now whisk in the white wine vinegar and cornflour/cornstarch.

Using a spatula, spoon the mixture onto the baking parchment on the baking sheet and spread into a disc shape the size of a dinner plate. Create a saucer-sized dip in the middle of the meringue, so that it will form a sort of bowl for the filling once cooked.

Bake in the preheated oven for 1 hour, then, without opening the door, turn the oven off. Leave the meringue in the oven for a further 2 hours, until completely cool. If you prefer, you can leave it in the oven overnight.

Once the pavlova base has cooled, remove it from the oven and carefully lift from the baking parchment – place onto a serving stand or plate.

Whisk the double/heavy cream and 1 tablespoon of the icing/confectioners' sugar until quite thick, then fold in the yogurt.

Lightly crush half of the raspberries with 1 tablespoon of icing/confectioners' sugar and fold into the cream. Spoon into the hollow of the base and gently spread out.

Pile the strawberries and remaining raspberries onto the cream.

Halve the passion fruits and squeeze the seeds out over the top of the pavlova. Decorate with a few sprigs of fresh mint and an extra dusting of icing/confectioners' sugar before serving.

Inclusion for those with additional dietary requirements has always been a core value at 2 Oxford Place. 'Well, that's obvious, it's a gluten-free restaurant,' you might say. But we try to go further than just offering gluten-free. Many of our customers also have a co-occurring dairy intolerance and we have a growing number of vegan diners. When we reveal to our dairy-free and vegan customers the separate dessert menu for them, they are always over the moon. This recipe doesn't compromise on creaminess or comfort. It's easy peasy to make and every bit as delicious as rice pudding made with dairy. Served with jam/jelly, it's the ideal end to a winter supper or, in our house, a Sunday lunch.

From start to serve: 1½–2 hours | Prep: 5 minutes | Cook: 1–1½ hours | Difficulty: ●○○○○

rice pudding

100 g/½ cup pudding/short-grain rice

50 g/¼ cup caster/granulated sugar

700 ml/2¾ cups unsweetened almond milk

1 teaspoon ground nutmeg

raspberry jam/jelly, to serve

an ovenproof casserole dish greased with dairy-free spread

SERVES 4–6

Preheat the oven to 180°C (350°F) Gas 4.

Put the pudding rice into the bottom of the prepared casserole dish.

In a jug/pitcher, stir together the sugar and almond milk, and pour over the rice. Give everything a stir, then sprinkle with the ground nutmeg.

Bake in the preheated oven for 1–1½ hours, stirring after 45 minutes and checking every 15 minutes thereafter.

Remove from the oven when the rice pudding is thick and creamy underneath with a papery skin on the surface.

Allow to cool slightly before serving with raspberry jam/jelly on the side.

We serve an elderflower fizz cocktail at the restaurant, which is the inspiration for this recipe. It's a delightfully light end to a meal and looks particularly elegant when adorned with fresh redcurrants. Add a sprinkle of popping candy just before serving for extra fizz. If you prefer not to include alcohol, substitute sparkling white grape juice or lemonade.

From start to serve: 3 hours | Prep: 15 minutes | Difficulty: ●○○○○

elderflower fizz jelly

250 ml/1 cup Prosecco

2 sheets large-leaf gelatine (if using small-leaf gelatine, use 4 pieces)

100 ml/6$^{1}/_{2}$ tablespoons elderflower cordial

100 g/$^{2}/_{3}$ cup fresh raspberries

GARNISHES (OPTIONAL)

redcurrants

popping candy

MAKES 3–4

Pour the Prosecco into a jug/pitcher and get the serving glasses ready – I like to use flutes, but you can use tumblers, small wine glasses or lightly oiled dariole moulds, so you can turn the jellies out of onto a plate before serving.

Fill a large bowl with water and fully submerge the gelatine sheets. Set aside to soften.

Put the elderflower cordial and 50 ml/3 tablespoons of water into a small saucepan and bring to a simmer over a medium heat. Remove the pan from the heat. Lift the gelatine sheets out of the water, give them a squeeze and then drop into the hot elderflower liquid. Stir until melted.

Pour the elderflower mixture into the jug/pitcher with the Prosecco and stir well. Set aside for a couple of minutes to cool slightly.

Place a few raspberries into each glass, stir the jelly mix again and pour into the glasses over the berries.

Push any fruit that pops up over the jelly back into the liquid so everything is fully submerged and put the glasses into the fridge to set for 2–3 hours. (During the first 30 minutes, you could check and prod the fruit down into the jelly so that the berries are suspended in the mixture when set.)

For added pizzazz, drape a bunch of reducrrants over the top of the glass and sprinkle a little popping candy onto the surface of the jelly to serve.

I like to think of cobbler as Stateside crumble. It's a fabulous summer dessert, and easy to whip up. Use really ripe peaches, or nectarines if you prefer, and serve with cream, custard or ice cream. You can vary the fruits if you like as well – an apricot or blackberry version are both utterly delicious.

From start to serve: 1 hour | Prep: 15 minutes | Bake: 40–50 minutes | Difficulty: ●○○○○

peach cobbler

8 large, ripe peaches

50 g/^{1}/$_4$ cup caster/granulated sugar

1 tablespoon plain/all-purpose gluten-free flour

1 teaspoon lemon juice

pouring cream, to serve

COBBLER TOPPING

260 g/1^3/$_4$ cups plain/all-purpose gluten-free flour

60 g/^{1}/$_4$ cup plus 1 tablespoon caster/granulated sugar

16 g/4 teaspoons baking powder

^{1}/$_2$ teaspoon xanthan gum

a pinch of salt

150 ml/^{2}/$_3$ cup natural yogurt

60 g/4 tablespoons unsalted butter, melted

2 eggs, beaten

a 20-cm/8-inch round baking pan

SERVES 4–6

Preheat the oven to 190°C (375°F) Gas 5.

Halve and stone the peaches and thinly slice them. Toss in a bowl with the caster/granulated sugar, flour and lemon juice, then spread evenly over the base of the baking dish.

Bake in the preheated oven for 10–15 minutes.

For the cobbler topping, mix together the flour, sugar, baking powder, xanthan gum and a pinch of salt in a large bowl. Make a well in the centre of the mixture and pour in the natural yogurt, melted butter and three-quarters of the beaten eggs (reserve one quarter for glazing the top of the cobbler). Stir everything together until it comes together in a wet dough and set aside for a minute or so.

Remove the peaches from the oven, give the cobbler topping another stir and then dollop 6–8 large spoonfuls of the mixture onto the fruit, spacing evenly apart. The topping will spread as it bakes, so all of the fruit doesn't need to be covered.

Lightly brush the tops of the dough with the remaining beaten egg and return the dish to the oven to bake for 30–35 minutes until the cobbler is golden and feels firm when gently pressed.

Remove from the oven and allow to cool for a few minutes before serving with cream.

For a cold-weather dessert, little can top sticky toffee pudding. Unapologetically sweet, and enriched with an obligatory caramel sauce, this is perfect served after a long, chilly, walk. This recipe harks back to the original method from the 1970s and avoids water-bathing or stove-top steaming. Rather than individual puddings, the sponge is baked separately from the caramel sauce.

From start to serve: 2 hours | Prep: 30 minutes | Bake: 45–50 minutes | Difficulty: ●●●○○

sticky toffee pudding

300 g/10 oz. (about 2 cups) chopped dried, stoned/pitted dates

1/2 tablespoon bicarbonate of soda/baking soda

115 g/7 1/2 tablespoons unsalted butter, softened

75 g/1/3 cup soft light brown sugar

200 g/1 cup caster/granulated sugar

4 eggs

200 g/1 1/3 cups plain/all-purpose gluten-free flour

10 g/2 1/2 teaspoons baking powder

a pinch of salt

custard, cream or ice cream, to serve

TOFFEE SAUCE

100 g/6 1/2 tablespoons unsalted butter

120 g/2/3 cup soft light brown sugar

150 g/2/3 cup double/heavy cream

a 20-cm/8-inch square cake pan lined with baking parchment

SERVES 6–9

Preheat the oven to 170°C (325°F) Gas 3.

Put the dates in a large pan and add enough water to just cover them completely. Bring the dates to the boil over a medium heat, then reduce the heat and allow to simmer for 10 minutes until softened.

Remove the pan from the heat and cool slightly. Add the bicarbonate of soda/baking soda, then, using a stick blender, blitz until no large pieces of date remain. Set aside.

In a large bowl, or the bowl of a free-standing mixer, cream the butter and sugars until pale. Add the eggs, flour, baking powder and salt, and beat until a thick, smooth batter is formed. Add the date purée and beat until combined. The batter will seem quite liquid at this stage, which is exactly as it should be.

Pour the mixture into the prepared cake pan and cover with a double layer of foil, tucking over the edges of the pan to seal.

Bake in the preheated oven for 30 minutes, then carefully remove the foil. (Don't worry if the top of the sponge has touched it during baking and a little comes off.) Return the cake to the oven and bake for another 15–20 minutes until the top of the cake springs back when lightly pressed and a skewer inserted into the centre comes out without any wet batter on it. Put the pan onto a wire rack and allow to cool slightly. Portion into 6–9 individual pieces of equal size.

For the toffee sauce, put the butter, sugar and cream into a heavy-bottomed saucepan and set over a low heat. Melt the ingredients together, stirring to prevent the sugar catching and burning on the bottom of the pan. Turn up the heat and bring to the boil. With a watchful eye, allow the sauce to bubble away for 3–4 minutes until thickened. The sauce should coat the back of a metal spoon. Be very careful not to touch the sauce, as it is extremely hot at this stage. Remove from the heat and allow to cool.

To serve, place a piece of the sponge into a dish and drizzle with plenty of warm caramel sauce. Accompany with custard, cream or ice cream.

Although not quite accurate, this recipe is named for its chameleon-like adaptability. It can be any flavour you want it to be. This recipe offers ideas for a few variations, but the list is almost endless. The only rule is to avoid adding anything that is going to limit the gelatine, such as pineapple, kiwi or alcohol.

From start to serve: 4 hours | Prep: 20 minutes | Difficulty: ●●○○○

chameleon cheesecake

300 g/10 oz. gluten-free digestive biscuits/graham crackers (see Note)

175 g/1½ sticks unsalted butter, melted

3 sheets large-leaf gelatine (if using small-leaf gelatine, use 6 sheets)

600 g/20 oz. full-fat cream cheese

80 g/⅔ cup icing/confectioners' sugar

1 vanilla pod/bean

350 ml/1½ cups double/heavy cream

VARIATIONS (OPTIONAL)

100 g/⅔ cup fresh raspberries or blueberries

150 g/⅔ cup chocolate hazelnut spread, lemon curd or dulce de leche

a 20-cm/9-inch springform cake pan

SERVES 8

To begin, make the cheesecake base. This is most easily done using a food processor; put the biscuits/crackers into it and whizz until they are in fine crumbs. Pour in the melted butter and mix until completely combined. (You can also make the base by hand by placing the biscuits in a plastic food bag wrapped in a kitchen cloth and bashing with a rolling pin to a crumb consistency.) Press the mixture evenly into the bottom of the pan and put in the fridge while you make the top of the cheesecake.

When you are about to make the topping, put the gelatine sheets in a bowl of cold water, ensuring that they are completely submerged, and set aside.

To a large bowl, or the bowl of a free-standing mixer, add the cream cheese and icing/confectioners' sugar. Remove the seeds from the vanilla pod/bean and add to the bowl. This is done by splitting open the pod/bean lengthways and carefully running the blade of a knife along the inside of each half. Whisk together the ingredients until well combined.

Warm the cream in a pan until simmering, then lift the gelatine leaves from the water, squeeze off the excess liquid and add to the cream. Remove the pan from the heat and stir to dissolve. Pour the cream and gelatine mixture into the cream cheese and whisk again, firstly on a slow speed, then increase the speed for 1–2 minutes until everything is well mixed.

Take the base from the fridge and pour the topping onto it. Return to the fridge and leave to set, which will take at least 3 hours.

If you have one to hand, removing the cake from the pan to serve will be made much easier by using a chef's blowtorch. Simply heat the outside of the pan all the way around for a few moments before releasing the springform fastening.

Note If you can't find digestives/graham crackers, any plain gluten-free biscuit/cookie will work here. If you are using an unsweetened cracker-style biscuit, add a few tablespoons of caster/granulated sugar before the melted butter.

Variations Try adding fresh raspberries or blueberries to the mixture once the topping has been well mixed. Or add chocolate hazelnut spread, lemon curd or dulce de leche before topping the base.

Making a roulade can be a fun challenge for any baker. Cracking is inevitable and it's usually nothing a good dusting of icing/confectioners' sugar won't fix. Making meringue roulade is more forgiving than working with gluten-free sponge cake, so if you are nervous about rolling a Yule Log (see page 138), give this one a go first to practice the techniques involved.

From start to serve: 2 hours | Prep: 20 minutes | Bake: 25-30 minutes | Difficulty: ●●●○○

raspberry and redcurrant roulade

5 egg whites

275 g/1^1/$_3$ cups caster/granulated sugar

1 teaspoon white wine vinegar

1 teaspoon cornflour/cornstarch

2 tablespoons icing/confectioners' sugar, plus extra for dusting

300 ml/1^1/$_4$ cups double/heavy cream

200 g/1^1/$_3$ cups fresh raspberries

150 g/1 cup fresh redcurrants

a Swiss/jelly roll pan lined with baking parchment

SERVES 8–12

Preheat the oven to 200°C (400°F) Gas 6.

In a spotlessly clean bowl, whisk the egg whites until they are stiff. Add the sugar, a heaped tablespoon at a time, whisking until fully incorporated. Once all the sugar has been added, the meringue should be very thick and shiny – now whisk in the white wine vinegar and cornflour/cornstarch.

Using a spatula, spoon the mixture onto the baking parchment on the Swiss/jelly roll pan and spread out evenly. Bake in the preheated oven for 10 minutes, then, without opening the door, turn the heat down to 170°C (325°F) Gas 3 and bake for a further 15–20 minutes until crisp and firm.

Remove the pan from the oven and leave to cool for 10 minutes.

Take a chopping board larger than your pan and lay onto it a clean kitchen cloth followed by a fresh piece of baking parchment. Dust the top of the meringue in the pan with icing/confectioners' sugar and then place the board over the pan so that the parchment meets the meringue. Invert the whole thing, then place onto a worksurface and carefully lift away the pan. Allow to cool completely.

When the meringue has cooled, whisk the double/heavy cream and the 2 tablespoons of icing/confectioners' sugar until quite thick, then fold in most of the raspberries. Strip half of the redcurrant berries from their stalks and fold these in as well.

Remove the parchment from the underside of the meringue and spread the cream and berry mixture evenly over the top.

Use the kitchen cloth and baking parchment to roll the meringue into a log shape – try to do so quite tightly, and don't worry if it cracks a little. Transfer to a serving plate or board and chill in the fridge before serving.

To serve, garnish the top of the roulade with the remaining raspberries and redcurrants and dust generously with icing/confectioners' sugar.

This has to be one of the simplest desserts to make, and as such it's perfect for days when you are pushed for time. I like to serve these in vintage china tea cups and garnish them with some candied lemon zest, but you can use small ramekins or even some pretty glasses if you'd prefer.

From start to serve: 3½ hours | Prep: 15 minutes | Cook: 15–20 minutes | Set: 3 hours | Difficulty: ●○○○○

lemon posset

3 large lemons
400 g/1³/4 cups double/
heavy cream
125 g/²/3 cup caster/
granulated sugar

CANDIED PEEL
1 lemon
70 g/¹/3 cup caster/
granulated sugar

MAKES 4

Finely zest 1 lemon and put the zest into a saucepan along with the cream and sugar.

Juice all of the lemons (including the one that has been zested) and set to one side, ensuring that there are no pips in the juice.

Over a low heat, bring the cream, sugar and lemon zest to a simmer for 2 minutes. Remove from the heat and whisk in the lemon juice.

Divide the mixture evenly between 4 tea cups, glasses or ramekins. Put in the fridge and allow to set for a minimum of 3 hours before serving.

While the possets set, make the candied peel for decoration.

Peel the lemon rind in long strips and use a sharp knife to remove any white pith from the underside.

Slice into thin strips and put into a saucepan with the sugar and 200 ml/³/4 cup of water. Heat the mixture over a low heat, stirring just until the sugar is dissolved and then bring to a simmer.

Simmer for 15–20 minutes until the strips of zest are almost translucent and the liquid has reduced by at least two-thirds.

Remove the pan from the heat and use a fork to lift the zest strips from the pan. Spread onto a baking sheet or plate in a single layer and leave uncovered to cool and set.

When you are ready to serve, take a few strips of candied peel and arrange in a curl on top of the now set lemon posset.

The winter months can get quite repetitive, dessert-wise. If you have guests coming over, why not offer this seasonal adaptation of a summer classic instead? Make the mulled fruits up to 48 hours in advance.

From start to serve: 5 hours | Prep: 30 minutes | Bake: 3 hours | Difficulty: ●●○○○

mulled fruit pavlova

4 egg whites

225 g/1¼ cups plus 2 tablespoons caster/superfine sugar

1 teaspoon white wine vinegar

1 teaspoon cornflour/cornstarch

300 ml/1¼ cups double/heavy cream

2 tablespoons icing/confectioners' sugar, plus extra to dust

MULLED FRUIT

200 ml/1 scant cup red wine

75 g/⅓ cup caster/granulated sugar

zest and juice of 1 orange, plus extra zest, to decorate

3 whole cloves

1 star anise

1 cinnamon stick

2 plums, halved, stoned/pitted and cut into thirds

1 apple and 1 pear, peeled, cored and thickly sliced

150 g/1 cup fresh blackberries

100 g/⅔ cup fresh raspberries

a baking sheet lined with baking parchment

SERVES 8–10

First make the mulled fruit. Put the wine, sugar, orange zest and juice, as well as the spices into a pan and bring to a simmer over a low heat for 5 minutes. Use a slotted spoon to remove the cloves, anise and cinnamon stick, then add the plum, apple and pear pieces. Simmer for a further 5 minutes. Remove the pan from the heat and stir in the blackberries and raspberries, then set aside to cool completely.

Preheat the oven to 150°C (300°F) Gas 2.

In a spotlessly clean bowl, whisk the egg whites until they are stiff. Add the caster/superfine sugar, a heaped tablespoon at a time, whisking until fully incorporated. Once all the sugar has been added, the meringue should be very thick and shiny – now whisk in the white wine vinegar and cornflour/cornstarch.

Using a spatula, spoon the mixture onto the baking parchment on the baking sheet and spread into a disc shape the size of a dinner plate. Create a saucer-sized dip in the middle of the meringue, so that it will form a sort of bowl for the filling once cooked.

Bake in the preheated oven for 1 hour, then, without opening the door, turn the oven off. Leave the meringue in the oven for a further 2 hours, until completely cool. If preferred, you can leave the base in the oven overnight.

Once the base has cooled, remove from the oven and carefully lift from the baking parchment – place onto a serving stand or plate and set aside.

Whisk the double/heavy cream and icing/confectioners' sugar until quite thick, then spoon into the hollow of the base and gently spread out.

Pile the mulled fruit on top of the cream, drizzling over some of the syrup.

Decorate with a little extra orange zest and an extra dusting of icing/confectioners' sugar, if desired, before serving.

Packed with grown-up flavours, this is a great for a dinner party. It's typically made with sponge fingers, which aren't readily available in gluten-free form, so I use coffee sponge cake instead. I also further eschew tradition and use coffee liqueur to enrich the cream, but marsala or sweet dessert wine works too.

From start to serve: 10 hours | Prep: 45 minutes | Bake: 30–35 minutes | Difficulty: ●●○○○

tiramisù

250 ml/1 cup whole milk

2 tablespoons instant coffee granules

260 g/1^3/$_4$ cups plain/all-purpose gluten-free flour

12 g/1 tablespoon baking powder

^{1}/$_4$ teaspoon salt

^{3}/$_8$ teaspoon xanthan gum

250 g/1^1/$_4$ cups caster/granulated sugar

70 g/5 tablespoons unsalted butter, softened

15 g/1 tablespoon sunflower oil

2 eggs

450 g/1^3/$_4$ cups double/heavy cream

50 g/scant ^{1}/$_2$ cup icing/confectioners' sugar

250 g/1 cup mascarpone cheese

75 ml/5 tablespoons Tia Maria or coffee liqueur

250 ml/1 cup strong black coffee, cooled

75 g/2^1/$_2$ oz. dark/bittersweet chocolate

cocoa powder, to dust

2 x 900-g/2-lb. deep loaf pans, greased and lined with baking parchment

SERVES 8–10

Preheat the oven to 190°C (375°F) Gas 5.

Heat 50 ml/3^1/$_2$ tablespoons of the milk in a pan over a low heat until simmering and stir in the coffee granules until dissolved. Add the remaining milk, stir, transfer to a jug/pitcher and set aside to cool completely.

To a large bowl, or the bowl of a free-standing mixer, add the flour, baking powder, salt, xanthan gum, caster/granulated sugar and softened butter. Whether using a handheld electric whisk or a free-standing mixer, slowly mix until the mixture resembles fine breadcrumbs.

Add the oil and eggs to the coffee-infused milk.

Continuing to mix the dry ingredients on a slow speed, pouring in the egg and milk mixture. Once combined, turn the speed to medium and mix for 3–5 minutes until the batter thickens. Divide the batter between the loaf pans and level with the back of a spatula or spoon.

Bake in the preheated oven for 30–35 minutes until slightly risen and the tops spring back when pressed lightly. Put the pans onto a wire rack and cool completely. Lift the sponges from the pans. Level the tops using a serrated knife and slice each cake in two horizontally.

Fully line one of the loaf pans with a double layer of clingfilm/plastic wrap.

Lightly whisk the cream with the icing/confectioners' sugar and add the mascarpone. Whisk until combined and quite thick, then add the Tia Maria, folding in with a spatula or metal spoon.

To assemble, pour the coffee into a shallow dish and quickly dip in one of the sponge pieces. Flip over so both sides soak up a little coffee, but don't allow it to become soggy. Put the sponge into the bottom of the lined loaf pan and spread over one-quarter of the marscapone cream in a smooth layer. Grate over one-third of the dark/bittersweet chocolate, then repeat the process with the remaining layers of sponge, cream and chocolate. Finish with a cream layer on top, but don't add any chocolate shavings.

Put in the fridge for at least 8 hours. When ready to serve, dust the top generously with sifted cocoa powder. Lift from the pan using the clingfilm/plastic wrap to help you, then slice to serve, revealing the layers inside.

This is a slight misnomer, as it's actually a scone and butter pudding, but you can make it with bread if you have that leftover instead. Making the pudding with scones means that sultanas/golden raisins are already incorporated into the mixture, but you can add a handful if using bread. If you have time, allow it to sit in the fridge for a few hours, or overnight, to allow the cream to soak into the scones, making the whole dish richer and more luxurious once baked.

From start to serve: 2 hours | Prep: 10 minutes | Bake: 30–35 minutes | Difficulty: ●○○○○

chocolate chip bread and butter pudding

3 Classic Scones (see page 26)

150 g/10 tablespoons unsalted butter, melted

50 g/^{1}/$_3$ cup dark/bittersweet chocolate chips

1 egg

50 g/^{1}/$_4$ cup caster/granulated sugar

^{1}/$_2$ teaspoon vanilla extract

100 ml/^{1}/$_2$ cup whole milk

100 ml/^{1}/$_2$ cup double/heavy cream

a 18 x 12-cm/7 x 5-inch baking dish, lightly greased

SERVES 2–3

Slice each scone into 6. Dip each slice into the melted butter until fully coated and arrange the slices, standing up, in the baking dish in overlapping rows.

Sprinkle over the chocolate chips, pushing between the scone pieces in places.

In a jug/pitcher, whisk together the egg, sugar and vanilla extract. Whisk in the milk and cream until well combined.

Pour the mixture over the scones, pushing the scone pieces gently with your hands to help encourage them to absorb the liquid.

Allow to rest in the fridge for a couple of hours, or overnight if you can.

When ready to bake, preheat the oven to 190°C (375°F) Gas 5.

Bake the pudding in the preheated oven on a baking sheet for 30–35 minutes until it is golden brown on top and the cream is set.

Allow to cool slightly before serving – it is excellent with pouring cream or warm custard.

15 g/1 tablespoon sunflower oil

2 eggs

240 ml/1 cup whole milk

1 teaspoon vanilla extract

260 g/1^2/$_3$ cups plain/all-purpose gluten-free flour

12 g/1 tablespoon baking powder

^{1}/$_4$ teaspoon salt

^{3}/$_8$ teaspoon xanthan gum

250 g/1^1/$_4$ cups caster/granulated sugar

70 g/5 tablespoons unsalted butter, softened

100 g/^{2}/$_3$ cup fresh raspberries

200 ml/1 scant cup sherry

135 g/4^1/$_2$ oz. raspberry jelly/jello tablets or 1^1/$_2$ cups high-pectin jelly such as redcurrant, quince or crabapple

CUSTARD

4 egg yolks

1 tablespoon cornflour/cornstarch

75 g/^{1}/$_3$ cup caster/granulated sugar

seeds from 1 vanilla pod/bean

400 ml/1^2/$_3$ cups double/heavy cream

200 ml/^{3}/$_4$ cup whole milk

TO SERVE

500 ml/2 cups double/heavy cream

milk/semi-sweet chocolate

glacé cherries

a 20-cm/8-inch square baking pan, greased and lined with baking parchment

SERVES 8–10

An unabashedly retro dessert, and one that may elicit a raised eyebrow from foodie friends. Roll with the kitsch and I guarantee everyone will be tucking in with oohs and aahs. Start preparing this the day before it's required, to make the sponge cake and to allow the jelly to set overnight.

From start to serve: 26 hours | Prep: 45 minutes | Bake: 30–35 minutes
Difficulty: ●●●○○

sherry trifle

Preheat the oven to 190°C (375°F) Gas 5.

Put the oil, eggs, milk and vanilla extract into a jug/pitcher.

To a large bowl, or the bowl of a free-standing mixer, add the flour, baking powder, salt, xanthan gum, sugar and softened butter. Whether using a handheld electric whisk or a free-standing mixer, slowly mix until the mixture resembles fine breadcrumbs. Continue to mix on a slow speed and pour the wet ingredients into the dry. Once combined, turn the speed to medium and mix for 3–5 minutes until the batter thickens.

Pour the batter into the prepared baking pan and level with the back of a spatula or spoon. Bake in the preheated oven for 30–35 minutes until slightly risen, golden and the top springs back when pressed lightly. Put the pan onto a wire rack and allow to cool.

Once completely cold, lift the sponge from the pan. Cut into cubes using a serrated knife and place in the bottom of a large glass trifle dish, along with the raspberries. (You will only need about half of the sponge.)

Pour over the sherry and toss together with the sponge and berries so everything is coated; be quite gentle so as not to break up the sponge.

Make up the jelly/jello according to the packet instructions, or melt the high-pectin jelly in a saucepan over a low heat, and pour over the sponge layer. Pour carefully so as to not mix the two layers too much. Put in the fridge to set overnight.

The next day, make the custard. Whisk together the egg yolks, cornflour/cornstarch, sugar and vanilla seeds in a jug/pitcher. Heat the cream and milk together in a saucepan until just simmering and then pour over the egg mixture. Whisk and then pour back into the saucepan and return to a low heat. Cook for 5–10 minutes, stirring constantly, until thickened.

Allow the custard to cool slightly, then pour over the now set jelly. Let cool completely, then whip the cream to soft peaks. Spoon over the custard and chill in the fridge.

Before serving, grate over the chocolate and decorate with glacé cherries.

yule log

From start to serve: 4 hours | Prep: 30 minutes | Bake: 15–20 minutes | Difficulty: ●●●●○

5 eggs, separated

175 g/³/4 cup plus
2 tablespoons caster/
granulated sugar

50 g/¹/3 cup plain/all-
purpose gluten-free flour

50 g/¹/3 cup plus
1 tablespoon cocoa powder

FILLING

200 ml/1 scant cup double /
heavy cream

1 tablespoon cornflour/
cornstarch

1 tablespoon icing/
confectioners' sugar

TOPPING

140 g/1 stick plus
1 tablespoon unsalted
butter, softened

125 g/1 cup cocoa powder

375 g/3¹/4 cups icing/
confectioners' sugar, plus
extra for dustind

4–6 tablespoons whole milk

*a Swiss/jelly roll pan lined
with baking parchment*

SERVES 8–12

Preheat the oven to 190°C (375°F) Gas 5.

Use a handheld electric whisk or a free-standing mixer to whisk together the egg yolks with the caster/granulated sugar until thick and pale.

Sift together the flour and cocoa powder and gently fold into the whisked egg yolks.

In a separate, spotlessly clean bowl, and using a clean whisk, whisk the egg whites until they are stiff. Fold gently into the rest of the mixture. Once fully incorporated, pour the mixture into the Swiss/jelly roll pan and spread out gently with the back of a large spoon or spatula.

Bake in the preheated oven for 15–20 minutes until the cake feels spongy to the touch. Set the on a wire rack to cool.

Once cooled, take a chopping board larger than the pan and lay a clean kitchen cloth on top followed by a fresh piece of baking parchment. Place the board over the pan so that the parchment meets the cake. Invert the whole thing and put onto a work surface and carefully lift away the pan. Peel off the baking parchment.

For the filling, whisk all of the ingredients until quite thick, then spread over the sponge in an even layer.

Use the kitchen cloth and baking parchment underneath to roll the sponge into a log shape – try to do so quite tightly, and don't worry if it cracks a little. Chill in the fridge for an hour before completing.

For the topping, with a handheld electric whisk or free-standing mixer, slowly mix together the butter, cocoa powder and icing/confectioners' sugar until no large lumps of butter remain. Add the milk and as the mixture starts to come together, increase the mixing speed to high. Beat until smooth, soft and fluffy.

Take the chocolate roll from the fridge and place onto a serving board. Cut a piece from the end, on the diagonal, and position on the side to make a branch. Cover the entire yule log with the topping, smoothing on with a palette knife. Use a fork to create a wooden, bark-like texture, then put in the fridge to chill for another hour or so.

Before serving, dust with icing/confectioners' sugar; it will fall beautifully into the grooves of the topping, giving the impression of a snow-dusted branch.

This is quite a long process, and rolling the chocolate sponge can seem daunting, but fear not, any cracks will be neatly covered by the chocolate topping. It's a lovely traditional Christmas bake, symbolizing the large log that was brought into the house and burned for the duration of the festivities.

SAVOURY
BAKES

These make an excellent lunch, served warm from the oven. They are a novel accompaniment to a bowl of hot tomato soup; cold, they can be packed up for picnics. Cheddar is recommended here, but any hard cheese can be grated or crumbled into the mix, and the herbs and spices varied to complement it. Why not try stilton and chive, manchego and basil or add 1 tablespoon of caster/granulated sugar instead of the mustard powder and give Wensleydale and dried cranberries a whirl?

From start to serve: 50 minutes | Prep: 15 minutes | Bake: 15–20 minutes | Difficulty: ●●○○○

cheese and rosemary scones

225 g/1^{1}/$_{2}$ cups plain/all-purpose gluten-free flour

18 g/4^{1}/$_{2}$ teaspoons baking powder

^{1}/$_{2}$ teaspoon mustard powder

^{1}/$_{4}$ teaspoon salt

^{1}/$_{4}$ teaspoon xanthan gum

40 g/3 tablespoons unsalted butter, softened

60 g/2 oz. (about ^{3}/$_{4}$ cup) grated Cheddar cheese

2 tablespoons fresh rosemary leaves, finely chopped

140 g/^{1}/$_{2}$ cup plus 1^{1}/$_{2}$ tablespoons buttermilk

1 egg

1 beaten egg, to glaze

butter and red onion marmalade, to serve (optional)

a straight-edged cookie cutter, 5–6 cm/2–2^{1}/$_{4}$ inches in diameter

a baking sheet lined with baking parchment or a silicone baking mat

MAKES 4–6

Preheat the oven to 190°C (375°F) Gas 5.

To a large bowl, or the bowl of a free-standing mixer, add the flour, baking powder, mustard powder, salt and xanthan gum. Add the butter in small pieces. Either rub in by hand or on a slow speed until the mixture resembles breadcrumbs and no large lumps of butter remain. Stir in the grated cheese and half of the rosemary.

In a jug/pitcher, combine the buttermilk and whole egg, then pour into the dry mixture. Stir together using a large metal spoon or on a slow speed. Once you have a sticky dough, stop mixing.

Dust the work surface well with extra gluten-free flour and tip the dough onto it. Using your hands, briefly knead the dough and then gently press into a flat disc that's approximately 2–3-cm/1–1^{1}/$_{2}$-inches deep.

Stamp out scones from the dough using the cookie cutter. Push straight down and lift the cutter straight up, as twisting will prevent the scones from rising evenly in the oven.

Bring together the remaining dough and re-knead briefly, then stamp out more scones.

Transfer the scones to the baking sheet. Space them to allow for spreading and rising. Brush over the tops of the scones with the beaten egg to glaze, then sprinkle with the rest of the chopped rosemary.

Bake in the preheated oven for 15–20 minutes until risen, golden and firm to the touch. Gently lift a scone up from the sheet: the bottom should also be lightly browned and sound hollow when tapped. If required, return zto the oven for 3–5 minutes more.

Allow to cool slightly on a wire rack before serving with lashings of butter and perhaps some red onion marmalade. These scones are best eaten on the day they are made.

A great staple for lunch, needing nothing more than a simple green salad to accompany it. You can vary the filling in this bake to suit your mood and dietary preference. Keep the egg and cream mixture constant and try combinations of feta and black olive, Cheddar cheese and bacon, or spinach and asparagus.

From start to serve: 5 hours | Prep: 20 minutes | Bake: 1½–2 hours | Difficulty: ●●●○○

salmon and pea quiche

1 batch Shortcrust Pastry (see page 17), at room temperature (if you haven't taken the pastry from the fridge in advance, give it a 15–20 second blast in the microwave before kneading)

5 eggs

500 ml/2 cups double/heavy cream

1 teaspoon ground black pepper

2 teaspoons salt

2 tablespoons snipped fresh chives, plus extra to serve

125 g/1 cup frozen peas

125 g/4 oz. smoked salmon, chopped

simple mixed leaf and tomato salad, to serve (optional)

a 23-cm/9-inch round deep quiche pan, greased

SERVES 6–8

Preheat the oven to 190°C (375°F) Gas 5.

Lightly knead the room-temperature pastry on a clean, cool work surface. Lay a piece or overlapping pieces of clingfilm/plastic wrap larger than your pan onto the work surface and lightly dust with plain/all-purpose gluten-free flour.

Roll the pastry into a ball and place in the middle of the clingfilm/plastic wrap. Gently press it into a disc shape with your hands. Lay a second piece of clingfilm/plastic wrap over the top and roll out the pastry to a thickness of 5 mm/¼ inch in a roughly circular shape around 40–45 cm/16–18 inches in diameter.

Remove the top layer of clingfilm/plastic wrap, then gently lift and press the pastry into the pan, so the remaining clingfilm/plastic wrap is now on top of the pastry. Remove this and trim the excess pastry away.

Line the case with a piece of baking parchment, then cover with baking beans. Transfer to a baking sheet and blind bake in the preheated oven for 20 minutes. Remove the beans and parchment, then return the case to the oven to bake for another 5–10 minutes until golden. Remove the case from the oven and set aside.

Reduce the heat to 120°C (240°F) Gas ½.

In a jug/pitcher whisk together the eggs, cream, pepper, salt and chives.

Spread half of the frozen peas over the base of the quiche case, along with half of the smoked salmon. Pour the egg mixture into the pastry case and then sprinkle over the remaining peas and salmon.

Return the quiche, still on its baking sheet, to the oven and bake for 1–1½ hours until the filling is almost set but has a slight wobble to the centre. Remove from the oven and set the pan on a wire rack to cool for an hour.

Refrigerate for a minimum of 2 hours, or even better overnight, before carefully removing from the pan and slicing into generous wedges. The quiche can be served cold or the pieces warmed up slightly in the oven. Be sure to portion the quiche before warming, as it will be much easier to cut when it is more firmly set. Serve with a simple salad sprinkled with chives.

This is a lovely little recipe to have in your repertoire. With poppy seeds they make delightfully delicate little Parmesan thins that you can serve alongside drinks or, if you omit the poppy seeds, they are perfect for floating atop a bowl of French onion soup or garnishing a mushroom risotto.

From start to serve: 10 minutes | Prep: 5 minutes | Bake: 5 minutes | Difficulty: ●○○○○

parmesan and poppy seed crisps

120 g/4 oz. Parmesan cheese, finely grated

1–2 teaspoons poppy seeds

2 baking sheets lined with baking parchment or silicone baking sheets

MAKES 10–12

Preheat the oven to 200°C (400°F) Gas 6.

Mix the Parmesan and poppy seeds in a small bowl, then place heaped tablespoons of the mixture onto the prepared baking sheets, well spaced apart. Gently pat down with your fingers so the mixture forms discs of around 2.5–3 cm/1–1¼ inches.

Bake in the preheated oven for 4 minutes until the cheese is bubbling and golden on top.

Remove from the oven and set the baking sheets onto wire racks to cool completely before carefully lifting the crisps from the sheets using a palette knife to help you. Alternatively, you could cool them slightly but, while still a little warm, drape over an upturned glass to form small baskets to serve canapés in for a party.

These crisps are best eaten on the day they are made.

Variations If poppy seeds aren't your thing, you could omit them altogether or omit and sprinkle with freshly snipped chives just before baking. You could also try adding 1 teaspoon dried oregano or 1 teaspoon dried/hot red pepper flakes in place of the poppy seeds.

'Ale' and 'pie' are words those who don't eat gluten would typically have to avoid on a menu. But that needn't be the case at home, and this recipe showcases both. It's important to prepare your filling in advance for this bake. Its basis is a slow-cooked casserole, rich with beef and simmered on the stove for a few hours.

From start to serve: 5 hours | Prep: 30 minutes | Bake: 3 hours | Difficulty: ●●●○○

steak and ale pie

800 g/1 lb. 14 oz. casserole/chuck steak, in chunks

3 tablespoons plain/all-purpose gluten-free flour

2 teaspoons salt

2 teaspoons white pepper

2–3 tablespoons vegetable or olive oil

1 onion, chopped

2 garlic cloves, finely chopped

4 carrots, chopped

4 large celery stalks/ribs, chopped

a 330-ml/12-oz. bottle of gluten-free ale

1 tablespoon tomato purée/paste

1 tablespoon balsamic vinegar

400 g/1^2/$_3$ cups gluten-free beef stock

1 batch Hot Water Pastry (see page 17), refrigerated

1 egg, beaten

4 x 500-ml/17-oz. pie dishes

MAKES 4

To make the casserole filling, toss the steak pieces with the flour, salt and pepper. Heat 2 tablespoons of oil in a large lidded casserole dish or frying pan/skillet and fry the meat for a few minutes until browned on all sides. Remove with a slotted spoon and set aside.

Add the onion and garlic with a little more oil to the pan and sauté until the onion is soft. Stir in the remaining vegetables and cook for a few minutes longer, then lift out of the pan and set aside with the meat.

Deglaze the pan with a large glug of ale, scraping up any crusty bits from the bottom and stirring into the liquid. Add the remaining ale and bring to a simmer. Stir in the tomato purée and balsamic vinegar, then return the meat and vegetables to the pan. Pour over the stock and give everything a stir. Bring to the boil, turn down the heat, cover and simmer for 2 hours.

Remove the lid, stir the casserole and simmer for a further 30 minutes, uncovered, before removing from the heat and setting aside to cool for 1–2 hours. When the filling has cooled down and you're ready to bake the pies, preheat the oven to 200°C (400°F) Gas 6.

Take the pastry from the fridge. Divide into 8 pieces and roll each piece into a ball with your hands. Put all but one piece back into the fridge.

Lay a piece of clingfilm/plastic wrap onto the work surface. Put the pastry piece in the middle and lay a second piece of clingfilm/plastic wrap over the top. Roll out the pastry to an oval or circle larger than the pie dishes, to a thickness of 2–3 mm/^{1}/$_8$ inch. Remove the top layer of clingfilm/plastic wrap and, using the layer underneath to help you, lift and turn over the pastry into the pie dish to line it. Press gently into the corners – try not to break it. Remove the clingfilm/plastic wrap, set aside and repeat.

Fill each lined dish with the cooled filling.

Take the remaining pastry from the fridge and repeat the rolling-out process to create 4 lids. Press the lid onto the overhanging pastry lining the dishes and then trim the excess with a sharp knife. Cut a small vent in the top of each pie dish and then brush the tops with the beaten egg.

Bake in the preheated oven for 25–30 minutes until golden and the filling is piping hot. Allow to cool for a few minutes before serving.

These tasty, vegetarian and dairy-free pasties are delicious served with a simple salad. Mango chutney on the side is also a lovely addition. You can adapt the filling to your preference, adding cheese or mushrooms or even some shredded roast chicken if you are a meat-eater. They are sturdy enough once cooled to be packed up and transported on journeys or picnics, but are quite delicate during the preparation process, so be careful when forming the shape and placing onto the baking sheets to avoid the pastry breaking – there's no need to panic, a small crack here and there won't affect them too much in the end.

From start to serve: 1 hour | Prep: 25 minutes | Bake: 15–20 minutes | Difficulty: ●●●○○

spiced lentil and spinach pasties

1 tablespoon olive oil

1/2 red onion, finely chopped

1 garlic clove, finely chopped

1 teaspoon cumin seeds

1 teaspoon dried chilli/hot red pepper flakes

1 teaspoon garam masala

1 teapoon salt

200 g/1 cup puy lentils, cooked

200 g/6 1/2 oz. spinach

1 batch Hot Water Pastry (see page 17), refrigerated

1 egg, beaten

a baking sheet lined with baking parchment or a silicone baking sheet

MAKES 5–6

Preheat the oven to 190°C (375°F) Gas 5.

To make the pasty filling, heat the oil in a saucepan and sauté the onion and garlic until the onion is soft. Add the spices and salt, stir and cook for 2 minutes more. Stir in the lentils and remove from the heat.

In another saucepan, wilt the spinach with a teaspoon of water and then drain, pushing the spinach onto a fine-mesh sieve/strainer to remove the excess liquid. Chop the spinach and stir into the lentils until evenly distributed and set aside to cool.

Take the pastry from the fridge. Break off a 100-g/3 1/2-oz. piece of pastry – weighing it out on the scales. Roll into a ball with your hands.

Lay a piece of clingfilm/plastic wrap onto the work surface. Place the pastry piece in the middle and lay a second piece of clingfilm/plastic wrap over the top. Roll out the pastry to a thickness of 4–5 mm/1/4 inch in a circle.

Remove the top layer of clingfilm/plastic wrap and place two tablespoons of the filling mixture into the middle of one side of the pastry disc.

Using the clingfilm/plastic wrap to help you, pull one side of the disc over the filling so that it meets the other side, forming a crescent shape.

Press down the edges to seal and trim away the excess. Crimp the edges lightly using a fork and then transfer to the lined baking sheet.

Repeat with the remaining pastry and filling, and once all the pasties are on the baking sheet, brush the tops with the beaten egg.

Bake in the preheated oven for 15–20 minutes until golden.

Remove and allow to cool for a few minutes before serving.

Baking a camembert is so simple to do, but is such a divine indulgence, especially with a good glass of red wine. Served with crunchy crudités, griddled asparagus spears and fresh grapes, it's a fantastic sharing appetizer or a simple supper. You could even add some toasted gluten-free bread, if you like.

From start to serve: 25 minutes | Prep: 5 minutes | Bake: 20 minutes | Difficulty: ●○○○○

baked camembert

250 g/8 oz. whole camembert

1 garlic clove

a few sprigs of fresh thyme

CRUDITÉS

1 large carrot, peeled and cut into batons

2 large celery stalks/ribs, cut into sticks

red grapes

a bunch of thick-spear asparagus

sea salt, to season

SERVES 2–4

Preheat the oven to 200°C (400°F) Gas 6.

Take the camembert from the box, remove the wrapping and then return to the box, leaving the lid off.

Cut the garlic clove in half and rub the surface of the cheese with the cut ends. Dot a few small sprigs of thyme into the top of the cheese.

Place the cheese, still in its box, onto a baking sheet and bake for 20–25 minutes in the oven until gooey all the way through.

While the camembert bakes, prepare the crudités and arrange on a platter with the grapes.

Snap the woody ends from the asparagus spears and put the asparagus into a pan of boiling water for 4 minutes, then drain.

Lightly oil and heat a griddle pan. When the pan is very hot, griddle the asparagus spears until lightly charred, sprinkle with sea salt and then serve on the platter alongside the cheese and other accompaniments.

Variations: You could serve this camembert just with fresh fruit as a warm alternative to a cheese board – try grapes, figs and sliced apple and pear. Omit the garlic and rosemary, drizzle with 1 tablespoon of honey and poke in a few sprigs of fresh lavender instead before baking. Or, for a spicier take, add a pinch of sea salt flakes and a 1–2 pinches of dried/hot red pepper flakes before baking.

It's always nice to see familiar favorites on offer and whenever there's a special-occasion buffet happening, I yearn for a mini sausage roll or two. Made with hot water pastry, which is easier to roll than shortcrust, you can make these with beef, lamb or even venison sausage meat, varying the seasoning to match. If you're after something vegetarian, you could try making a cheese and onion filling using sautéed onions, grated Cheddar cheese and parsley.

From start to serve: 1 hour | Prep: 20 minutes | Bake: 12–15 minutes | Difficulty: ●●○○○

sausage rolls

350 g/12 oz. sausage meat (if you can't find gluten-free sausage meat, remove the skins from gluten-free sausages, which are readily available)

2 tablespoons finely chopped fresh parsley

1 teaspoon ground black or white pepper

1 batch Hot Water Pastry (see page 17), refrigerated

1 egg, beaten

wholegrain mustard, to serve

a baking sheet lined with baking parchment or a silicone baking sheet

MAKES 16

Preheat the oven to 190°C (375°F) Gas 5.

In a bowl, or using a food processor on pulse setting, mix together together the sausage meat, parsley and pepper with 2 tablespoons of water until completely combined.

Take the pastry from the fridge and lightly knead on a clean, cool work surface. Lay a piece or overlapping pieces of clingfilm/plastic wrap onto the work surface. Place the pastry ball in the middle and lay a second piece of clingfilm/plastic wrap over the top. Roll out the pastry quite thinly in an oblong shape. The thickness should be only around 2–3 mm/^{1}/$_8$ inch.

Remove the top layer of clingfilm/plastic wrap and cut down the middle of the pastry lengthways so that you have two long rectangles.

Place the sausage meat in a thin roll running the length of the two pastry pieces – half of the filling on each.

Brush the long edge of one of the pastry pieces with the beaten egg, then gently lift and roll the pastry over the sausage filling, pressing it onto itself at the other side to form a tight seal. Trim the excess away and then roll the whole thing carefully so that it is cylindrical in shape and the seal is at the bottom. Repeat with the other pastry and filling.

Using a sharp knife, cut the rolls into 8 pieces, or more if you want really tiny sausage roll bites, then arrange on the prepared baking sheet.

Brush the tops with the remaining beaten egg and bake in the preheated oven for 12 minutes. Check the sausage rolls and if they are not yet golden and the sausage cooked through, return to the oven for a couple more minutes. Remove from the oven and cool slightly before serving with wholegrain mustard on the side.

These sausage rolls are best eaten on the day they are made, but can be prepared in advance and stored, uncooked, in the fridge, covered with clingfilm/plastic wrap, baking just before you need to serve them.

suppliers and resources

The ingredients in this book can mostly be found at larger supermarkets, including online delivery services. For anything that you can't find, try the following suppliers, websites and use the Coeliac UK and Celiac Disease Foundation (US) resources online.

UK

2 Oxford Place
www.2oxfordplace.com
+44 (0)113 234 1294
To learn more about our completely gluten-free restaurant, visit us in Leeds or online.

Cake Craft Shop
www.cakecraftshop.co.uk
+44 (0)1732 463 573
For baking equipment, decorating supplies and food colours.

Coeliac UK
www.coeliac.org.uk
+44 (0)333 332 0233
For more information on coeliac disease.

Doves Farm
www.dovesfarm.co.uk
+44 (0)1488 684880
Organic flour specialists with a range of gluten-free flours, baking powder and xanthan gum.

Gluten Free Foods Ltd.
www.glutenfree-foods.co.uk
+44 (0)20 8953 4444
For gluten-free treats like digestive biscuits/graham crackers.

Healthy Supplies
www.healthysupplies.co.uk
For a wide range of gluten-free flours, breads and breadcrumbs as well as other ingredients.

Koko Dairy Free
www.kokodairyfree.com
+44 (0)1564 731 980
For coconut yogurt and milk products.

Lakeland
www.lakeland.co.uk
+44 (0)15394 208 8100
For baking equipment, decorating supplies and food colours.

Real Foods
www.realfoods.co.uk
All-organic, natural-food retailer with a wide range of gluten-free flours and ingredients, as well as nuts and seeds.

Tobia Teff
www.tobiateff.co.uk
+44 (0)20 7018 1210
Quality supplier of teff flour.

Whole Foods Market
www.wholefoodsmarket.com
+44 (0)20 7368 6100
Supermarket for free-from produce.

US

Bob's Red Mill
www.bobsredmill.com
+1 (800) 349-2173
For gluten-free wheat and teff flour, baking powder and xanthan gum.

Celiac Disease Foundation
www.celiac.org
+1 (818) 716-1513
For more information on celiac disease.

King Arthur Flour
www.kingarthurflour.com
+1 (800) 827-6836
For gluten-free flour, baking powder and xanthan gum

MI-DEL
www.midelcookies.com
For gluten-free treats like digestive biscuits/graham crackers.

Whole Foods Market
www.wholefoodsmarket.com
+1 (844) 936-2273
Supermarket for free-from produce.

index

A
ale: steak and ale pie 149
almond milk 10–11
    rice pudding 117
almonds
    Florentines 38
    frangipane 94
    marzipan 53, 78–9
    rocky road 33
apples
    apple crumble 113
    tarte tatin 97

B
Bakewell tart 94
baking powder 8
baking soda see
        bicarbonate of soda
banoffee pie 82
Battenberg cake 78–9
beef: steak and ale pie 149
bicarbonate of soda 8
biscuits
    brandy snaps 30
    party rings 34
biscuits, digestive
    banoffee pie 82
    chameleon cheesecake
        125
    key lime pie 90
    rocky road 33
brandy buttercream 54
brandy snaps 30
bread and butter pudding,
        chocolate chip 134
brownies 22
butter 8–9
buttercream 79
    brandy buttercream 54
buttermilk 9
    red velvet cake 63
butternut squash:
        pumpkin pie 89

C
cakes
    Battenberg cake 78–9
    cake truffles 37
    carrot cake 64
    Christmas cake 72
    cookie dough cake 67
    'malt' loaf cake 76
    red velvet cake 63

salted caramel cake 60–1
Victoria sponge cake 71
yule log 138–9
see also cupcakes; loaf
        cakes
camembert, baked 153
candied fruit 10
    lemon posset 129
caramel
    banoffee pie 82
    croquembouche 86
    millionaire's shortbread
        29
    salted caramel cake 60–1
cardamom: chocolate and
        cardamom tart 106
carrots
    carrot cake 64
    steak and ale pie 149
chameleon cheesecake 125
cheese
    baked camembert 153
    cheese and rosemary
        scones 142
    Parmesan and poppy
        seed crisps 146
cheesecake, chameleon
        125
cherries, glacé
    Christmas cake 72
    Christmas pudding 75
    florentines 38
    rocky road 33
cherry jam/jelly: cherry
        Bakewell cupcakes 53
chocolate 9
    banoffee pie 82
    brownies 22
    cake truffles 37
    chocolate and cardamom
        tart 106
    chocolate chip bread and
        butter pudding 134
    chocolate éclairs 105
    chocolate frosting 45
    chocolate hazelnut
        cupcakes 57
    chocolate sauce 19
    chocolate shortcrust
        pastry 17
    cookie dough cake 67
    double chocolate scones
        25

Florentines 38
millionaire's shortbread
        29
rocky road 33
tiramisù 133
yule log 138–9
choux pastry/paste
    chocolate éclairs 105
    croquembouche 86
Christmas cake 72
Christmas pudding 75
cobbler, peach 121
cocoa 9
coconut cream: coconut
        crème brûlée 110
coconut milk 10
    piña colada cupcakes 50
coffee: tiramisù 133
colours, food 9
condensed milk
    key lime pie 90
    millionaire's shortbread
        29
confectioners' sugar see
        icing sugar
cookie dough cake 67
cookies see biscuits
cornflour/cornstarch 10
crackers, Graham see
        biscuits, digestive
cream 9
    banoffee pie 82
    chameleon cheesecake
        125
    chocolate and cardamom
        tart 106
    chocolate éclairs 105
    croquembouche 86
    key lime pie 90
    lemon posset 129
    mulled fruit pavlova 130
    perfect pavlova 114
    raspberry and redcurrant
        roulade 126
    strawberries and
        cream cupcakes 42
    tiramisù 133
cream cheese
    chameleon cheesecake
        125
    cream cheese frosting 63
crème brûlée, coconut 110
crisps, Parmesan and

poppy seed 146
croquembouche 86
crudités 153
crumble, apple 113
cupcakes
    basic vanilla cupcakes 41
    cherry Bakewell cupcakes
        53
    chocolate hazelnut
        cupcakes 57
    lavender cupcakes 46
    lemon cupcakes 49
    mince pie cupcakes 54
    piña colada cupcakes 50
    spring nest cupcakes 45
    strawberries and cream
        cupcakes 42
custard 19
    egg custard tarts 93
    sherry trifle 137

D
dairy-free spreads 9–10
dates
    'malt' loaf 76
    sticky toffee pudding 122
dried fruit 10
    Christmas cake 72
    Christmas pudding 75
    'malt' loaf 76
    mince pies 102

E
éclairs, chocolate 105
eggs 10
    crème brûlée 110
    egg custard tarts 93
    lemon curd 18
elderflower fizz jelly 118
equipment 12

F
fish: salmon and pea
        quiche 145
Florentines 38
flour 10
frangipane 94
freezing cakes 13
frostings 14
    brandy buttercream 54
    brown sugar frosting 67
    buttercream 79
    chocolate frosting 45, 57

coconut frosting 50
cream cheese frosting 63
lavender frosting 46
lemon frosting 49
salted caramel frosting
    60–1
vanilla frosting 41
fruit
    mulled fruit pavlova 130
    see also apples; dried
        fruit, etc
fruit cakes
    Christmas cake 72
    'malt' loaf 76

G
glacé cherries
    Christmas cake 72
    Christmas pudding 75
    florentines 38
    rocky road 33
glaze, orange 64
golden raisins see sultanas

HI
hazelnuts: chocolate
    hazelnut cupcakes 57
hot water pastry 17
icing sugar 11
ingredients 8–11

JK
jam/jelly, raspberry 18
jars, sterilizing 4, 13
jelly, elderflower fizz 118
key lime pie 90

L
lavender cupcakes 46
lemons
    lemon cupcakes 49
    lemon curd 18
    lemon meringue tart 101
    lemon poppy seed drizzle
        loaf 68
    lemon posset 129
lentils: spiced lentil and
    spinach pasties 150
limes: key lime pie 90
loaf cakes
    lemon poppy seed drizzle
        loaf 68
    'malt' loaf 76

MNO
marshmallows, rocky
    road 33
marzipan
    Battenberg cake 78–9
    cherry Bakewell cupcakes
        53
mascarpone cheese:
    tiramisù 133
meringues
    lemon meringue tart
        101
    mulled fruit pavlova
        130
    perfect pavlova 114
    raspberry and redcurrant
        roulade 126
milk 10
millionaire's shortbread 29
mincemeat
    mince pie cupcakes 54
    mince pies 102
mixed peel
    Christmas cake 72
    Florentines 38
mulled fruit pavlova 130
nuts 11
oils 11
orange glaze 64

PQ
Parmesan and poppy seed
    crisps 146
party rings 34
pasties, spiced lentil and
    spinach 150
pastry
    hot water pastry 17
    shortcrust pastry 17
pavlova
    mulled fruit pavlova 130
    perfect pavlova 114
peach cobbler 121
peas: salmon and pea
    quiche 145
pecan nuts
    carrot cake 64
    pecan pie 85
pies
    mince pies 102
    steak and ale pie 149
piña colada cupcakes 50
poppy seeds

lemon poppy seed
    drizzle loaf 68
Parmesan and poppy
    seed crisps 146
posset, lemon 129
Prosecco: elderflower fizz
    jelly 118
pumpkin pie 89
quiche, salmon and pea
    145

R
raisins: Christmas pudding
    75
raspberries
    elderflower fizz jelly 118
    perfect pavlova 114
    raspberry and redcurrant
        roulade 126
    raspberry jam 18
    sherry trifle 137
raspberry jam/jelly:
    Bakewell tart 94
    sherry trifle 137
red velvet cake 63
redcurrants: raspberry
    and redcurrant roulade
    126
rice pudding 117
rocky road 33
rosemary: cheese and
    rosemary scones 142
roulade, raspberry and
    redcurrant 126
rum: piña colada cupcakes
    50

S
salmon and pea quiche 145
salt 11
    salted caramel cake 60–1
sauces
    chocolate sauce 19
    custard 19
    toffee sauce 122
sausage rolls 154
scones
    cheese and rosemary
        scones 142
    classic scones 26
    double chocolate scones
        25
seeds 11

sherry trifle 137
shortbread, millionaire's 29
shortcrust pastry 17
spices 11
spinach: spiced lentil and
    spinach pasties 150
spring nest cupcakes 45
steak and ale pie 149
sterilizing jars 4, 13
sticky toffee pudding 122
storage 13
strawberries
    perfect pavlova 114
    strawberries and cream
        cupcakes 42
sugar 11
sultanas
    carrot cake 64
    Christmas pudding 75
    classic scones 26
    'malt' loaf 76

T
tarts
    Bakewell tart 94
    chocolate and cardamom
        tart 106
    egg custard tarts 93
    lemon meringue tart 101
    tarte tatin 97
    treacle tart 98
tea: 'malt' loaf cake 76
techniques 14–15
teff flour 10
tiramisù 133
toffee: sticky toffee
    pudding 122
treacle tart 98
trifle, sherry 137
truffles, cake 37

VW
vanilla 11
    basic vanilla cupcakes 41
Victoria sponge cake 71
walnuts: Florentines 38

XY
xanthan gum 11
yogurt
    peach cobbler 121
    perfect pavlova 114
yule log 138–9

acknowledgments

No baker is an island and there are a great number of people who I would like to thank for their help in the creation of this book…

Firstly, thank you to all the lovely customers, past and present, you have been the inspiration for this collection of recipes. And to every one of my friends who supported me in transforming a fledgling cupcake business into a full-time job (and didn't point out the frosting in my hair).

To every member of the awesome team at Toxy HQ, it's such a pleasure to work with you all and thank you for your support during this process.

Thank you to my agent, Clare Hulton, for taking the time to listen to a dream and then guiding me through the process of making it a reality.

Huge thanks to everyone who has been involved in this book at Ryland Peters and Small. Special thanks to Cindy Richards and Julia Charles for taking a chance on a newbie. To Sonya Nathoo and Leslie Harrington, for the beautiful design of the book and for taking the time to make the process so inclusive. To Patricia Harrington, for the printed pages. And to Steph Milner, for the edits, long distance e-support and for remaining utterly unphased by receiving essays in the early hours.

Thank you to Adrian Lawrence, for photography and background tunes, and to his lovely assistants for strong and plentiful coffee. To Luis Peral, for gorgeous styling executed with passion and flair, and to Jack Sargeson for teaching me literally everything I know about food styling while creating great shots and great vibes.

The most heartfelt of thank yous to my parents, Arthur and Glenda Hall, as without 2 Oxford Place, this book wouldn't exist. Thank you for everything you have done to make the restaurant happen, which is more than I can say, and for a lifetime of love, support, life lessons and advice.

Last, but certainly not least, endless love and thanks to Jono, for keeping me sane, fed and watered through the writing days, for always believing in me and gallantly taste-testing everything that came your way. And, of course, to Tilly, for teaching me how to bake a tooth fairy cake – I promise to keep it a secret.